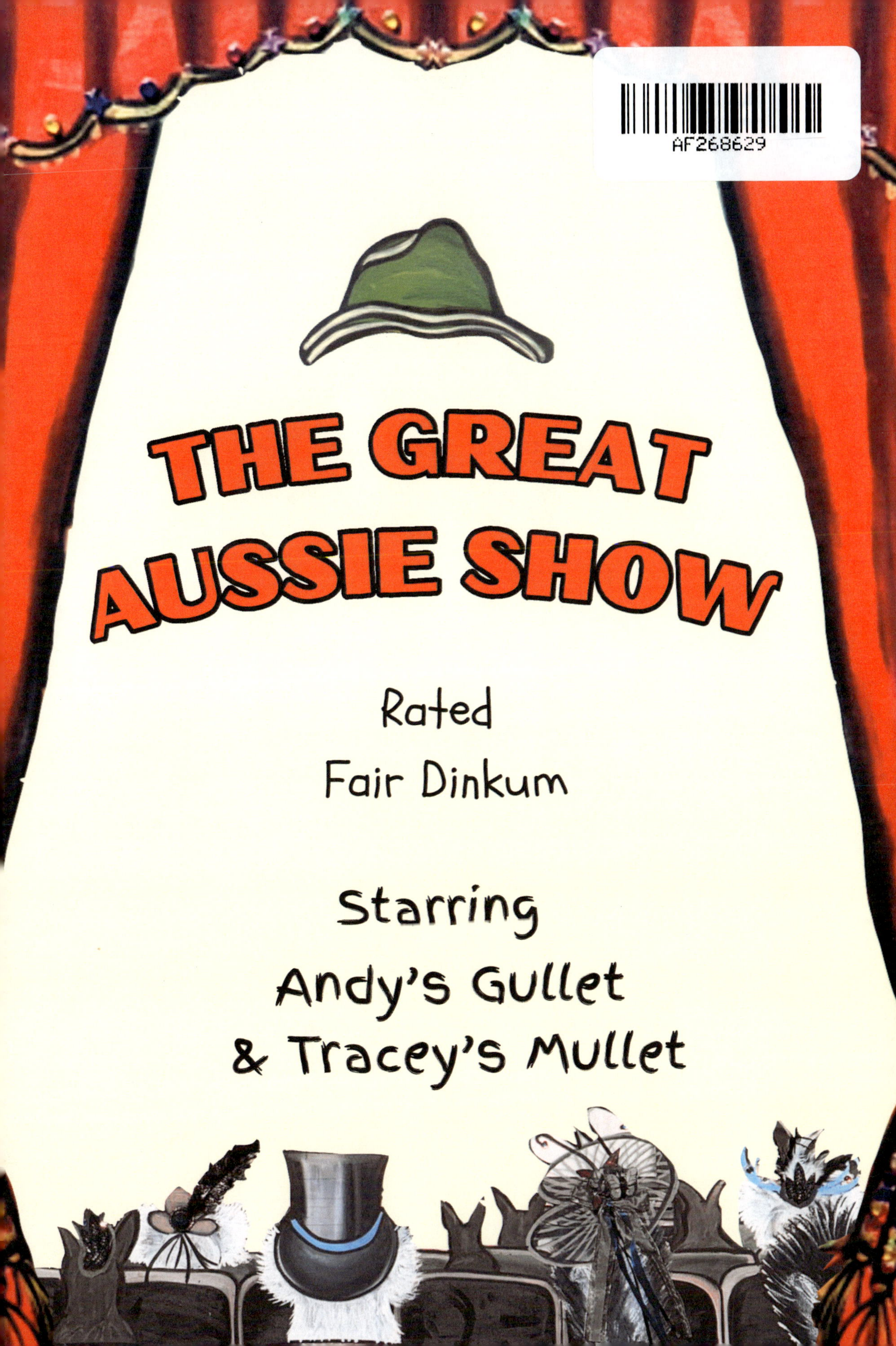

THE GREAT AUSSIE SHOW

Rated
Fair Dinkum

Starring

Andy's Gullet
& Tracey's Mullet

Title: The Great Aussie Show
ISBN: 978-1-7642790-1-7

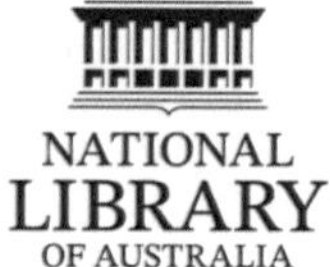
A catalogue record for this book is available from the National Library of Australia

First Published in Australia, somewhere near Woop Woop, by AyMate press, 2025

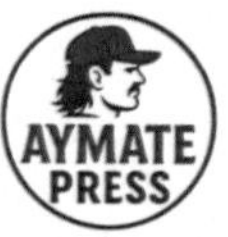

© Text: Andrew Skvorc, 2025
© Illustrations: Tracey Esteves, 2025

Search "Tracey Esteves Art" online to discover more of her artistic work beyond these pages.

Ahhh G'day...

It's kinda hard to tell yuz this but as me missus knows,
that when I talk in public an' all, me mates yell,"Stone the crows!"
It's coz I'm not the talkin' type, me mouth's forever shut,
but when I tell yuz what I saw, I swear I'm not a nut.

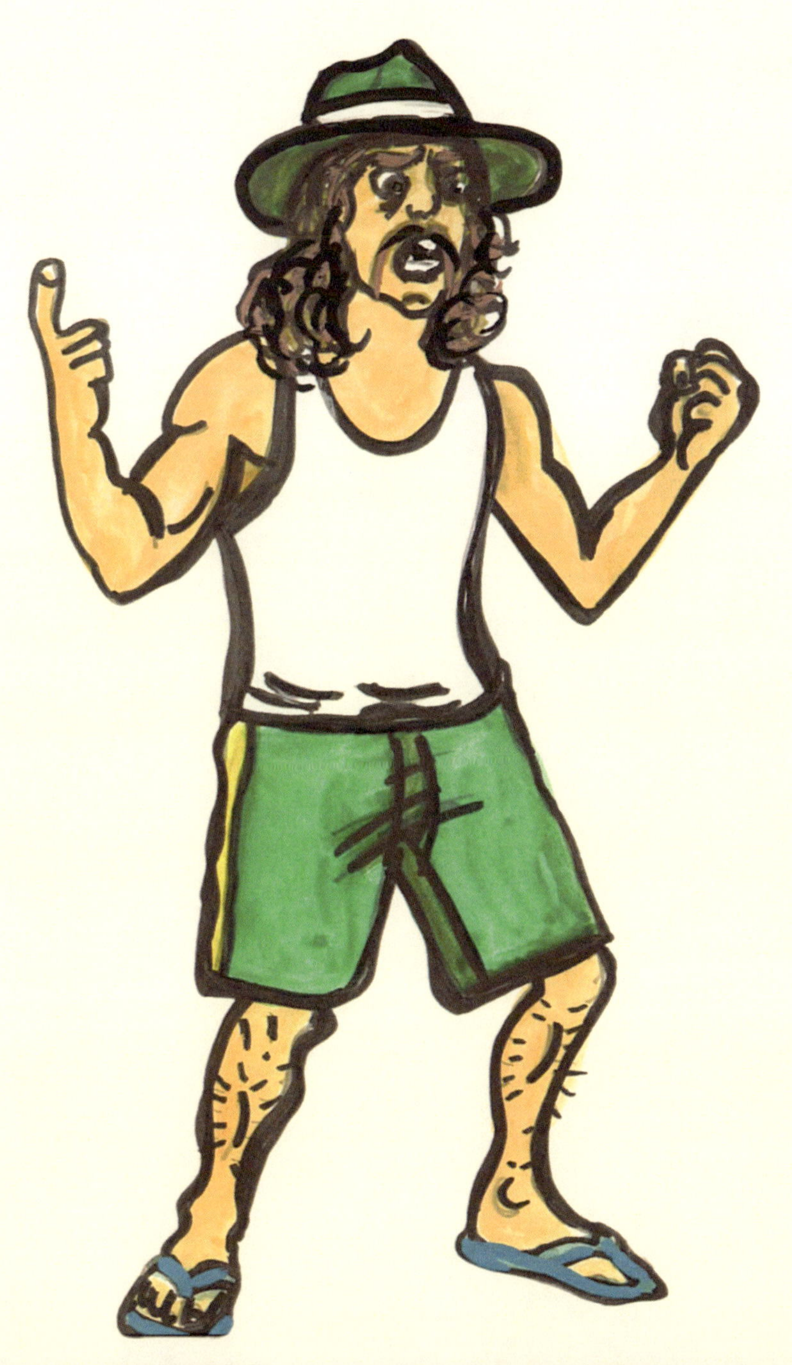

I spent the mornin' shakin' off me 'eadache from last night,
I tell yuz I done nuffin' wrong and didn't start no fight.
It's 'ard to know where to begin but I don't give a darn,
how flamin' dumb I'm gunna look, while tellin' yuz this yarn.

When walkin' inta town last night, while feelin' pretty crook,
I reckoned I'd feel better if I read meself a book.
I went into the lib-e-ry and this I'll let yuz know,
I saw a bunch o' animals about to watch a show.

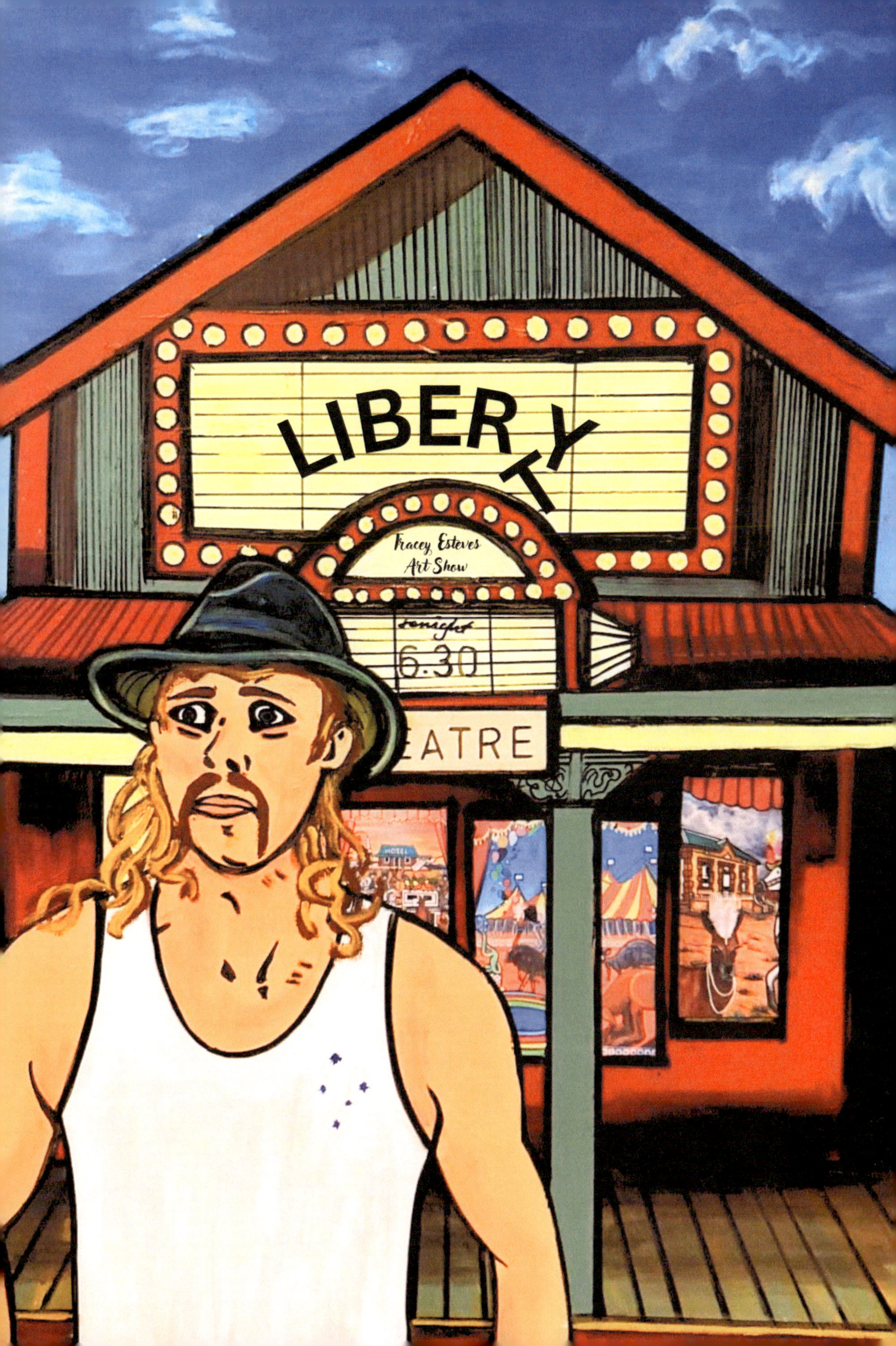

LIBERTY
Tracey Esteves
Art Show
Tonight
6.30
EATRE

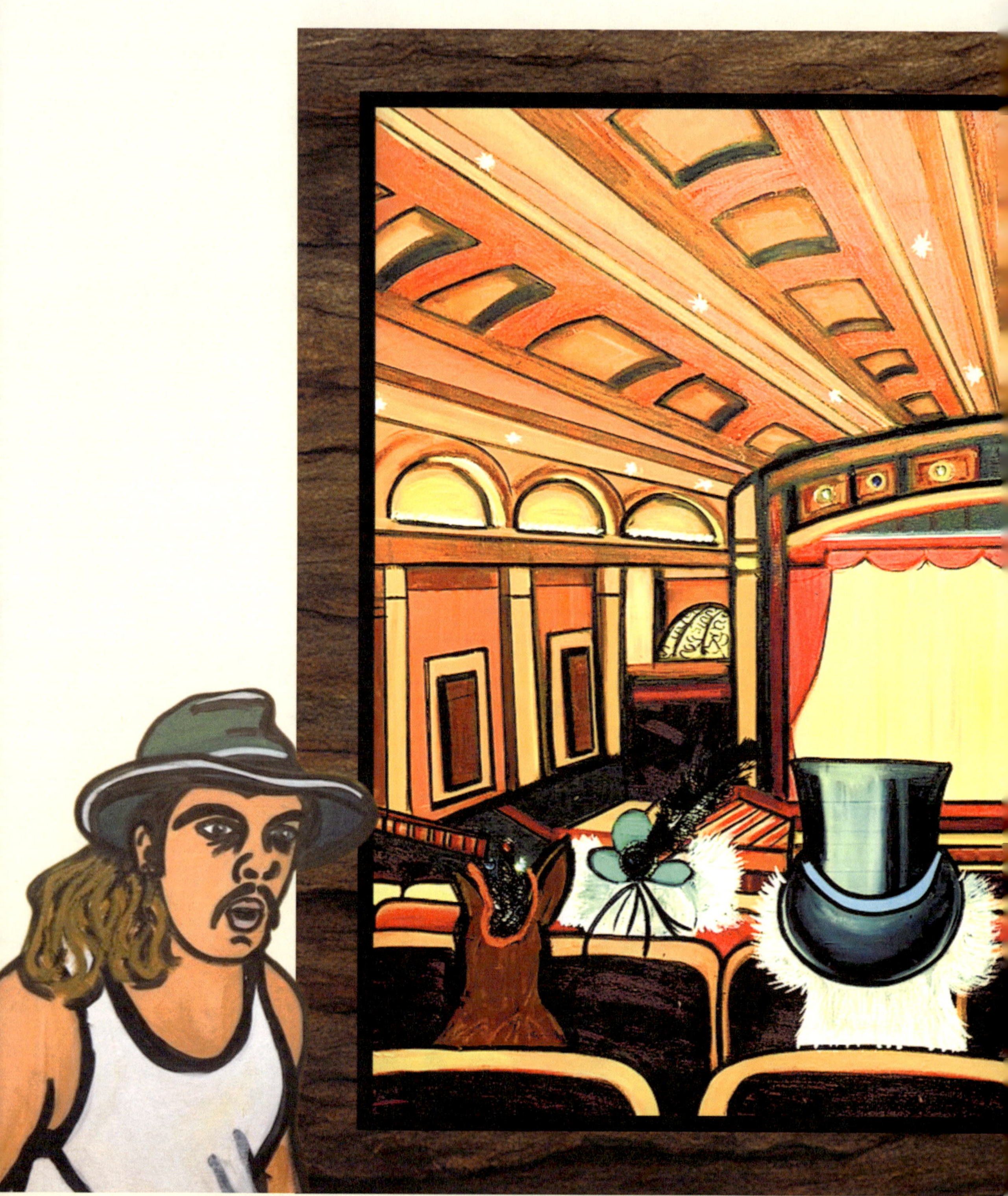

There sat a group o' kangaroos and one 'e 'ad a hat,
but that's not all I'm tellin' yuz, not leavin' it at that!
Two emus 'eads were pokin' up wiv 'ats on 'em as well,
and when I saw the two koalas, strewth I nearly fell.

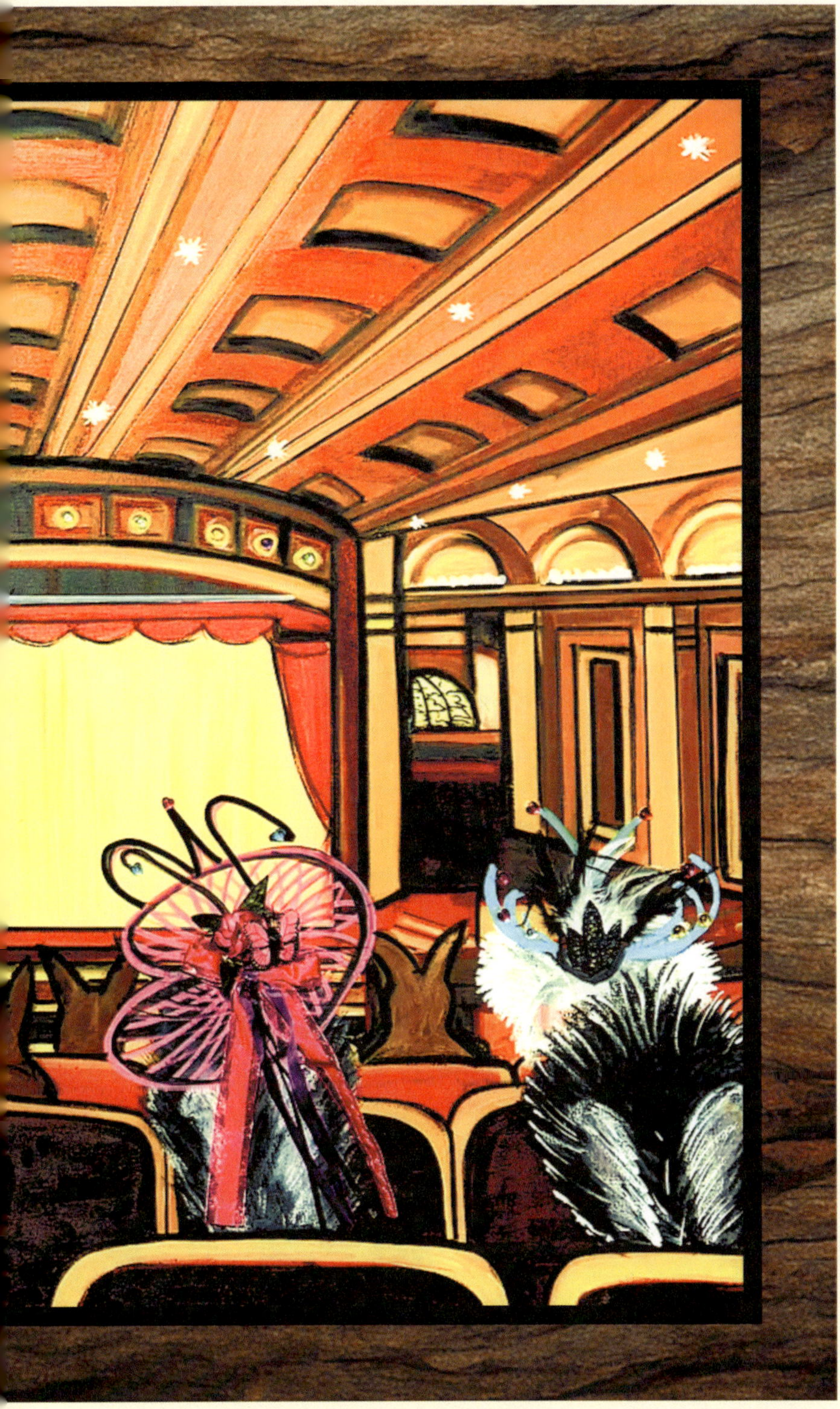

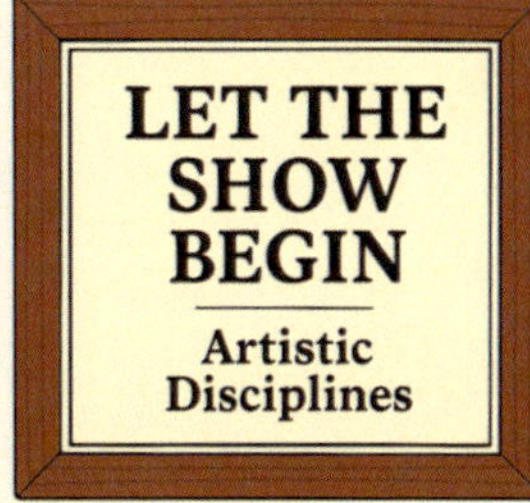

I wondered where the books were at, you'll find out in a sec,
I never thought I'd speak o' this, but now, well what the heck?
Me job was keeping clandestine, I checked from side ta side,
it's then I saw the big red curt'n swing right open wide.

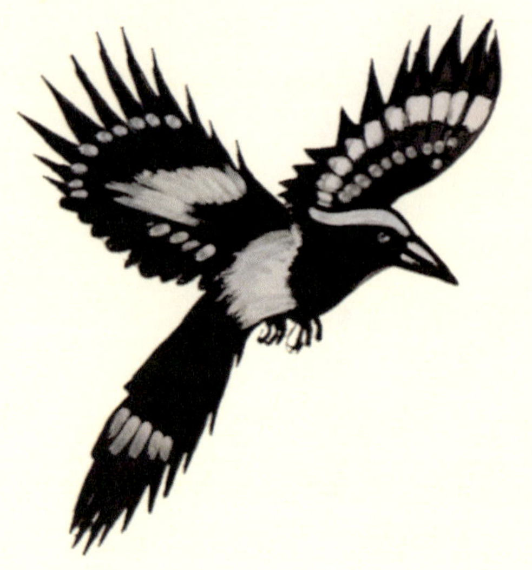

What 'appened next I kid ya not,
I know what youse are thinkin',
that maybe this is all a hoax an' I
spent the night up drinkin'.
But 'ear me out, I need the yack
ta get this off me mind,
be'ind that curt'n stood a bird,
the scary swoopin' kind.

Above its 'ead a cocky flapped
while holdin' onta paper,
and on the shelf a bilby sat,
just addin' to the caper.
Now standin' up in front o' them,
I 'adn't got a clue,
a giant rabbit readin' or a
well-dressed kangaroo?

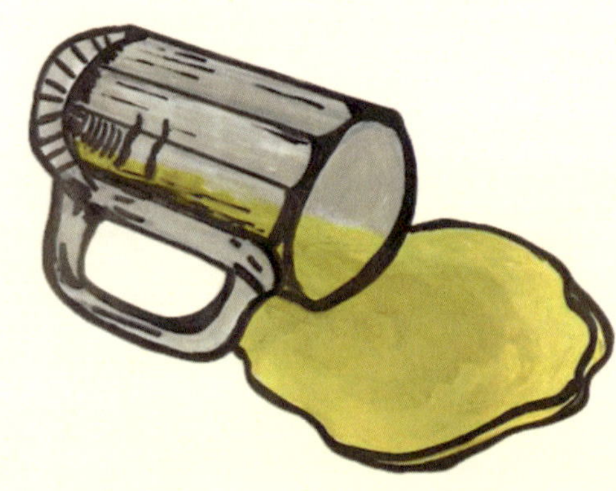

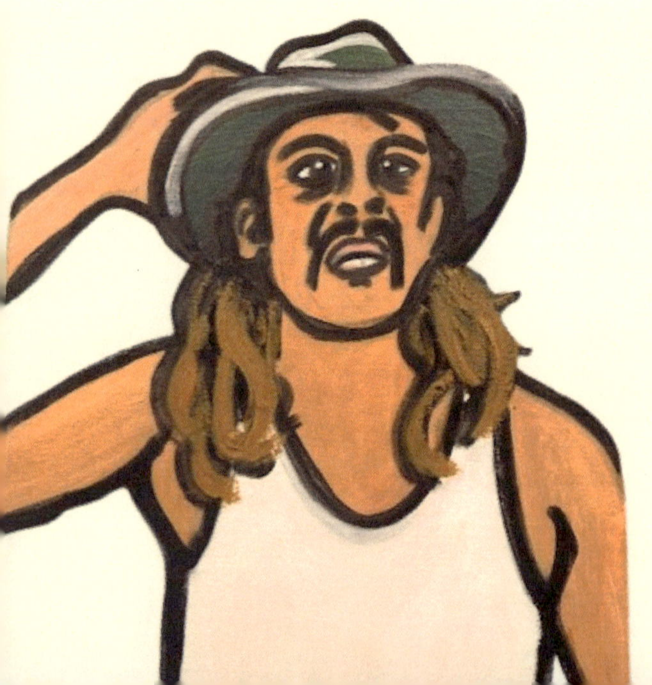

Now say yuz don't believe me,
because ev'ryfing is true,
a koala sitting next to 'em
wore clothes, like me and you.
Up a little 'igher was an
owl like lookin' fing,
a boobook's watchya call it and
'is 'oot 'as quite a ring.

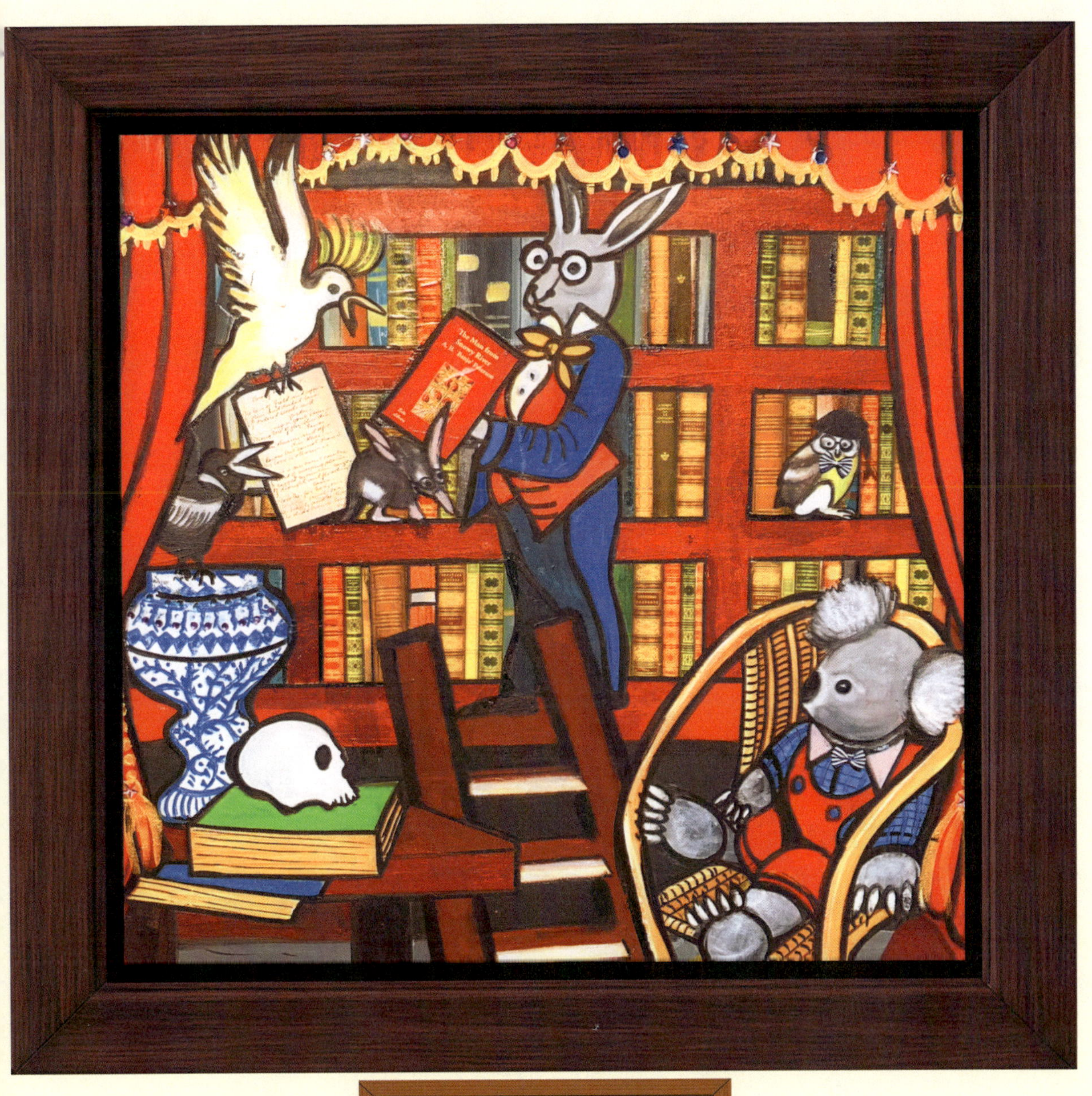

**KEEPER OF THE
BUSHLAND BOOKS**

Reading and Literature

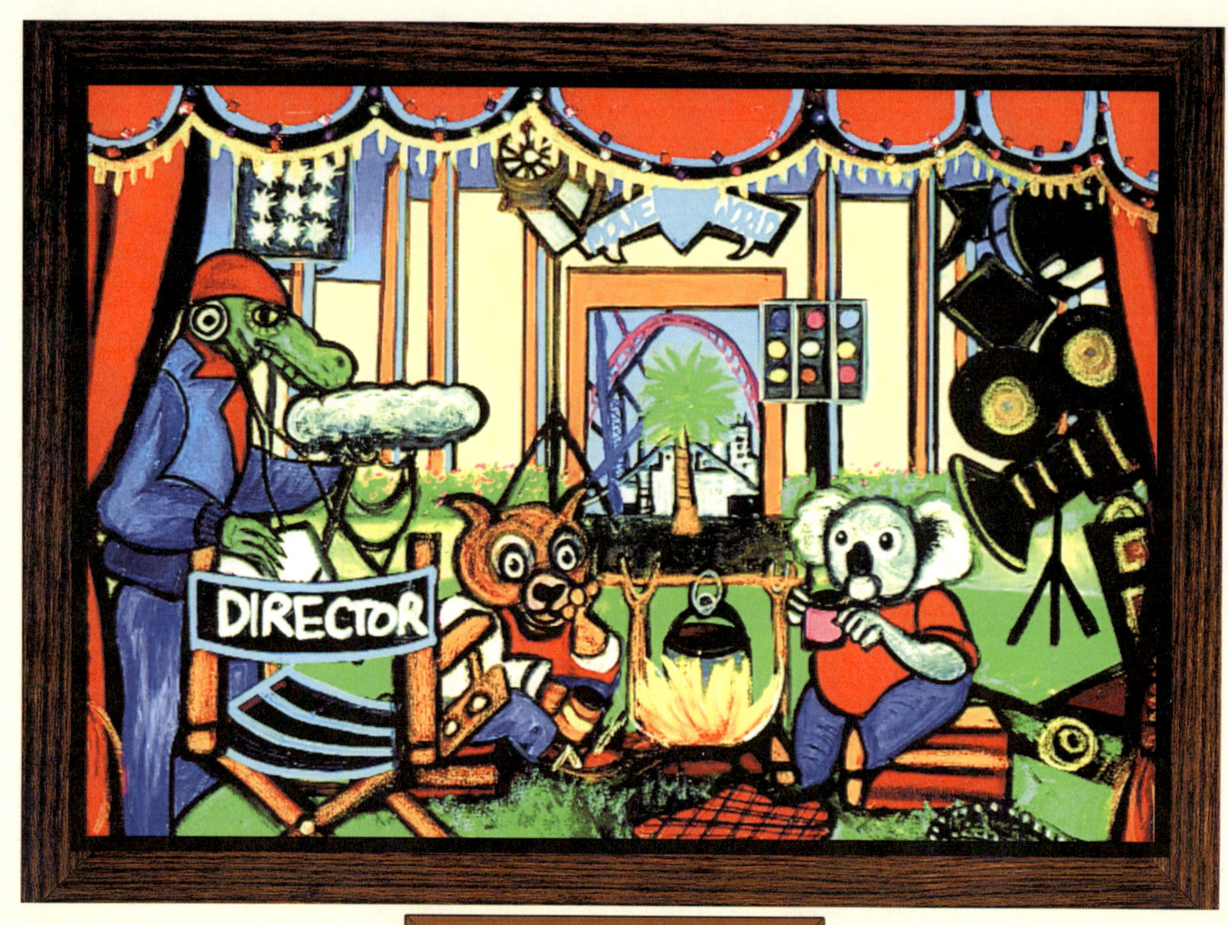

**THE WILDLIFE TAKE:
A CINEMATIC
ADVENTURE**
Cinema and Movie-making

Now bein' the sober type I am, as good as they can get,
believe me now as I explain the changin' of the set.
The curt'ns shut an' open'd up, it took me by surprise,
there sat a wombat drinkin' tea, with big and googly eyes.

Its mate was a koala, who was drinkin' tea as well,
both staring at a bush telly, as far as I could tell.
A croc was standin' to the left, I crept towards the door,
now if me wife asks where I woz, just tell 'er what I saw.

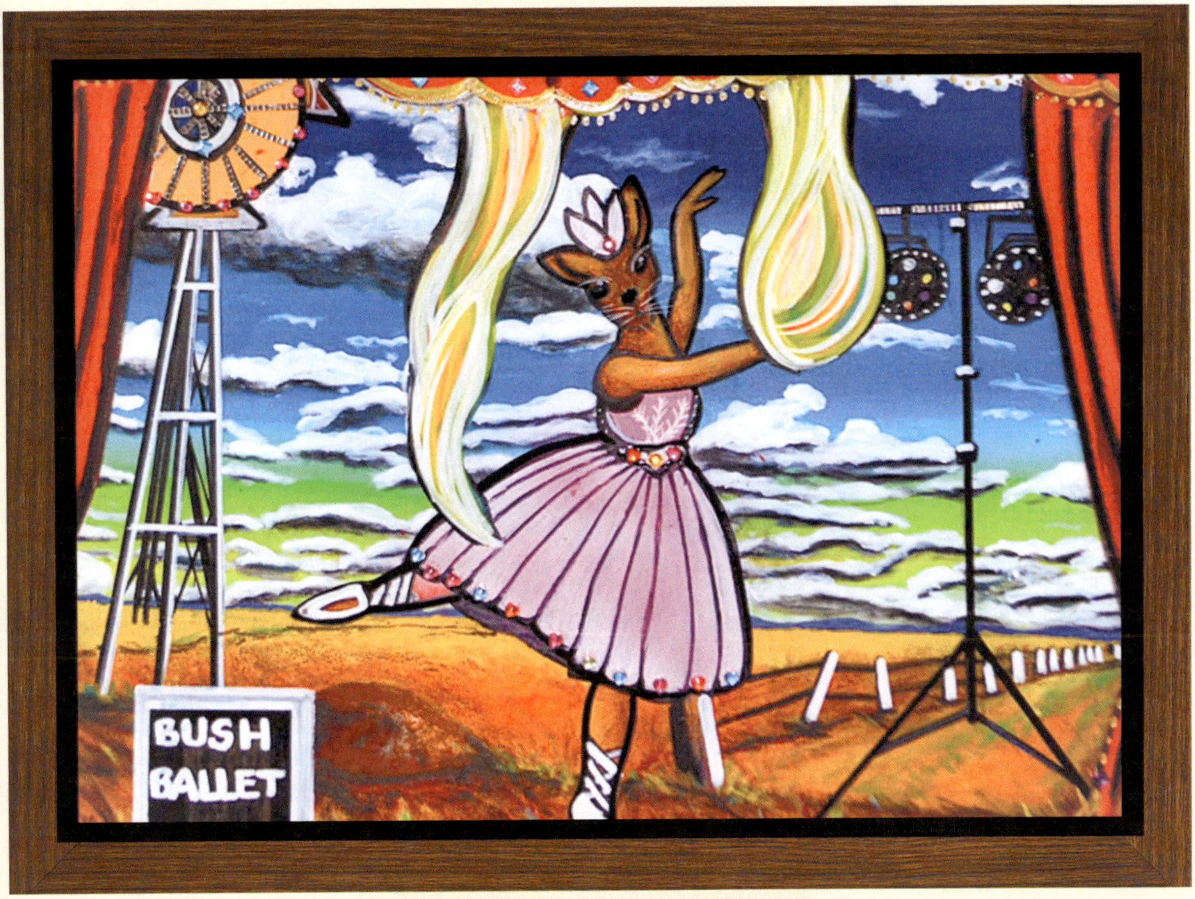

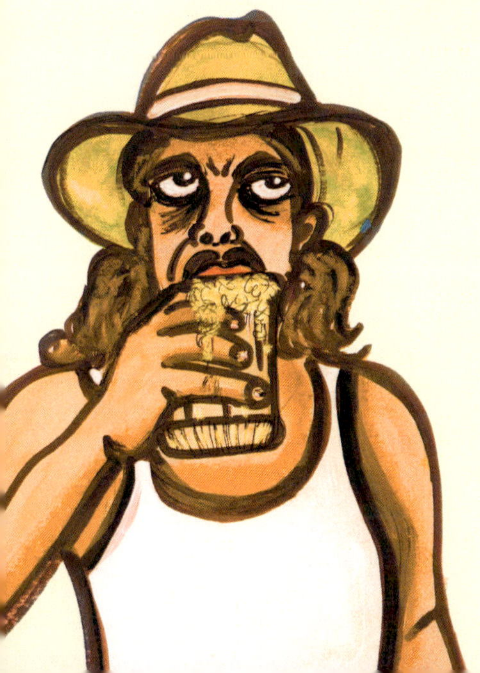

BUSH BALLET

—

Ballet

Yuz won't believe what came up next
and neeva will me missus,
a big red danced across the stage,
while blow'n me some kisses.
I thought I might be seein' things
so took a second look,
the curt'n shut then open'd with
a lanky lookin' chook.

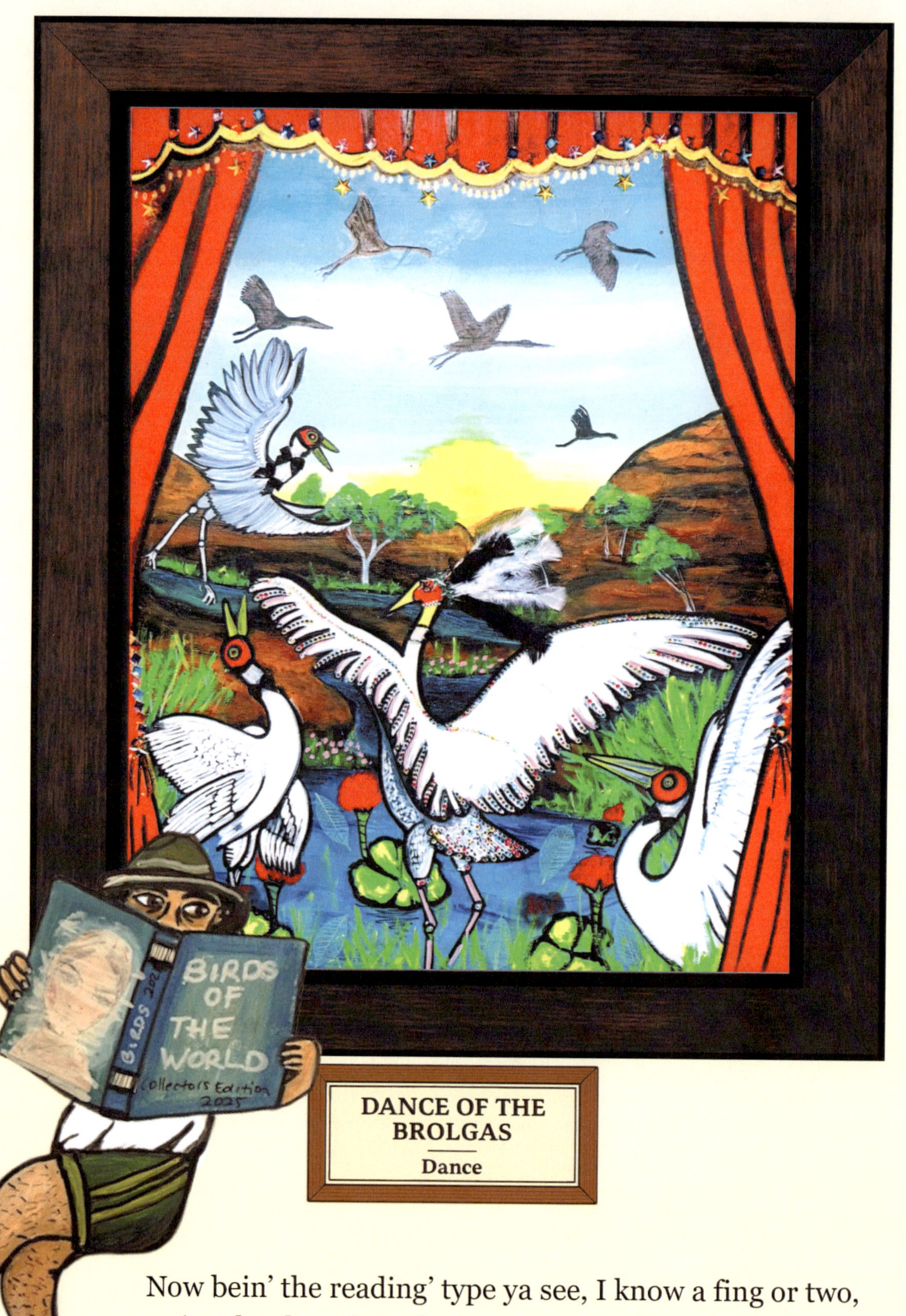

DANCE OF THE BROLGAS
Dance

Now bein' the reading' type ya see, I know a fing or two,
just let the missus know so we avoid another blue.
That this 'ere bird I seen last night is known by name as brolga,
been readin' on it all night long, not doin' nuffin' vulgar.

Up next I seen a dancin' troupe o' roos wi' special feet,
and right above their 'eads was perched a massive parakeet.
Now if me missus questions youse on this we shall agree,
in overalls I saw a grey koala in a tree.

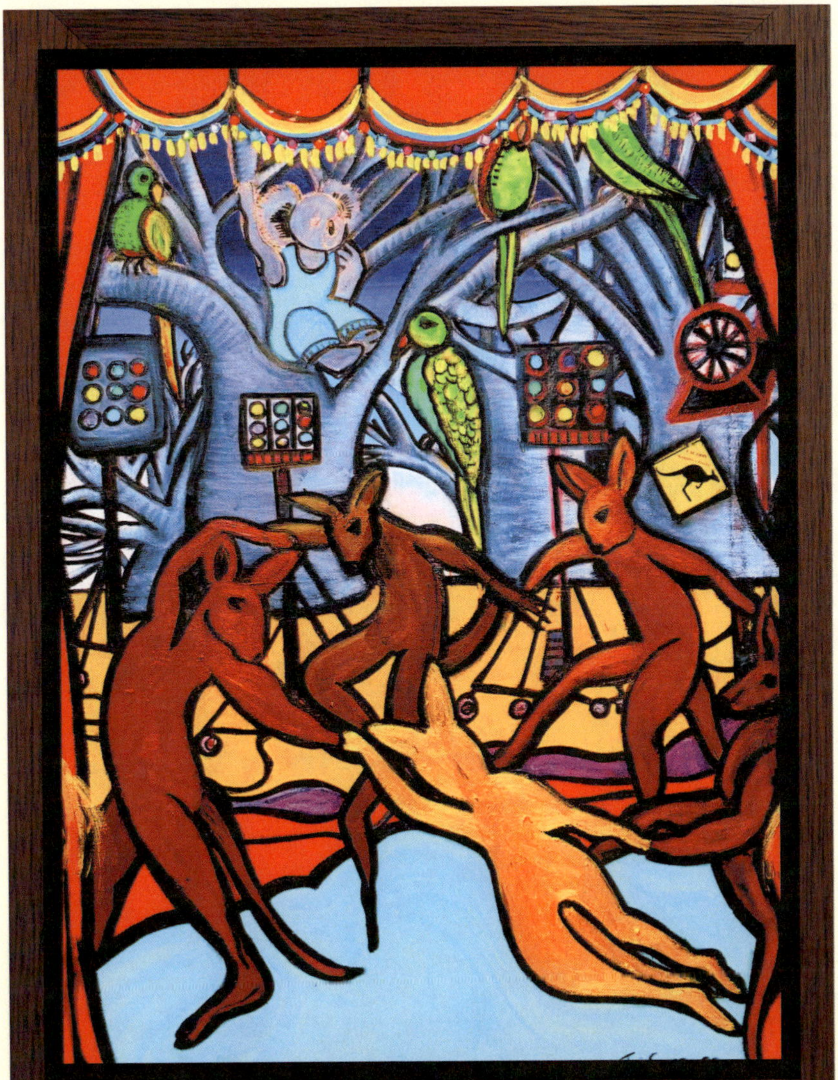

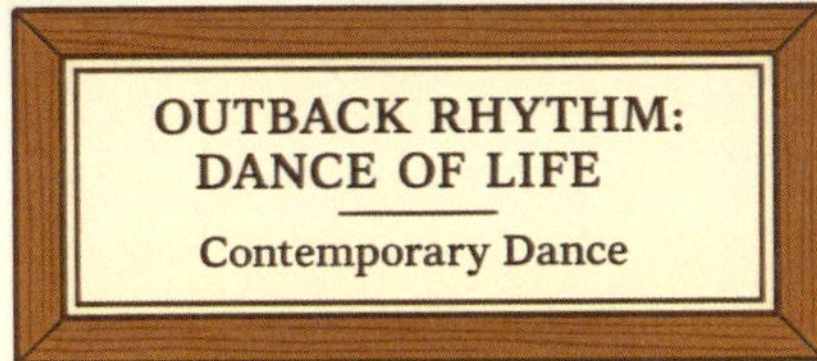

OUTBACK RHYTHM:
DANCE OF LIFE

Contemporary Dance

Now whaddaya reckon I tell ya some more,
so long as I cover me tracks.
If the missus finds out I done anyfing else,
there'd be skid marks all over me daks.

A cocky rocked up it was starin' at me,
lookin' sharp with 'is little bow tie.
It flew past a bus flappin' wings of its own,
as the wind made the Aussie flag fly.

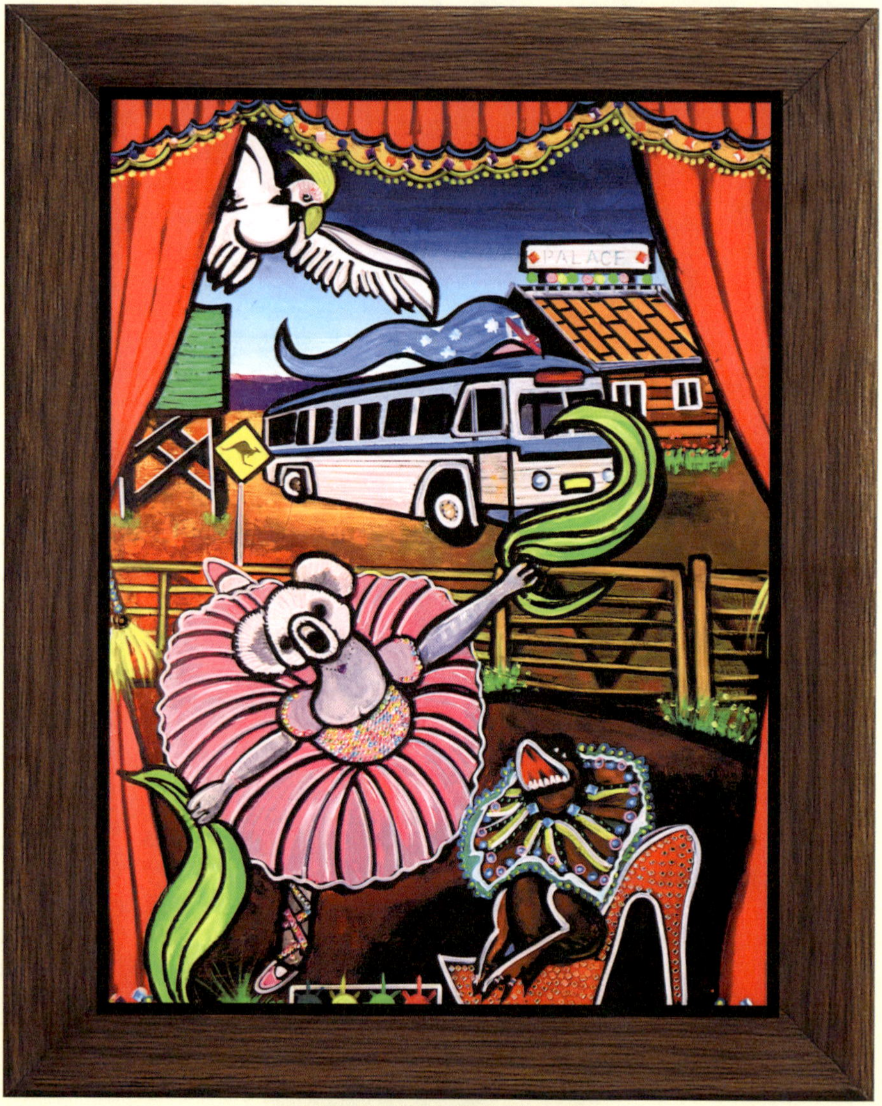

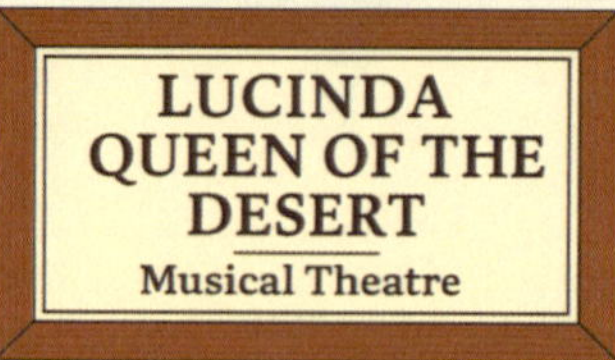

Now tell 'er I saw a koala just dancin',
on stage in a little tutu.
And sittin' right there with a frilly brown neck,
was a lizard atop of a shoe.

The whole fing is true I'm not tellin' a lie,
can ya make sure me missus finds out?
Coz I tried on the lizard shoe, hurtin' me toe,
and I swear that I 'aven't got gout.

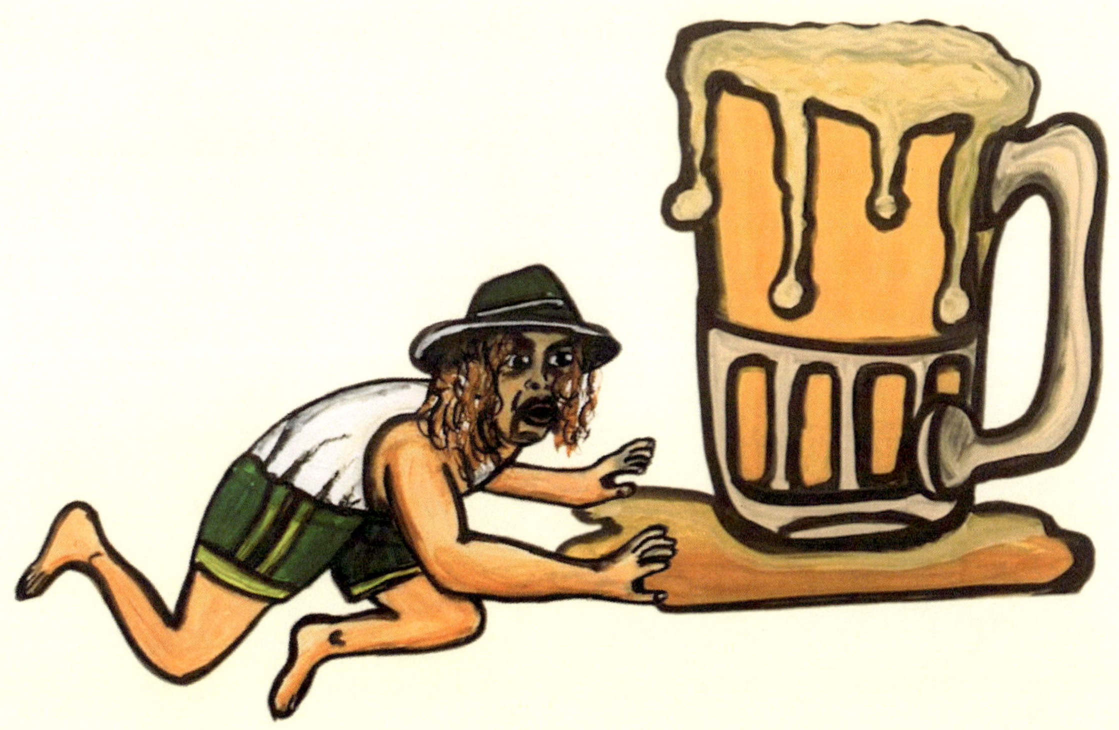

The next ya know the curtains shut, but this'll hit yuz for six,
what came up next was nuffin short of me mind playing dirty tricks.
I swung me 'ead and crooked me neck and that's what did me vertebra,
on stage it looked fair dinkum like an animal orchestra.

Two kookaburras on a mic
and one was on an 'arp,
what's more was three koalas
on their trumpets for a start.
With emus on guitars,
me foot was tappin' to the beats,
and singin' along the piano
were some rainbow lorikeets.

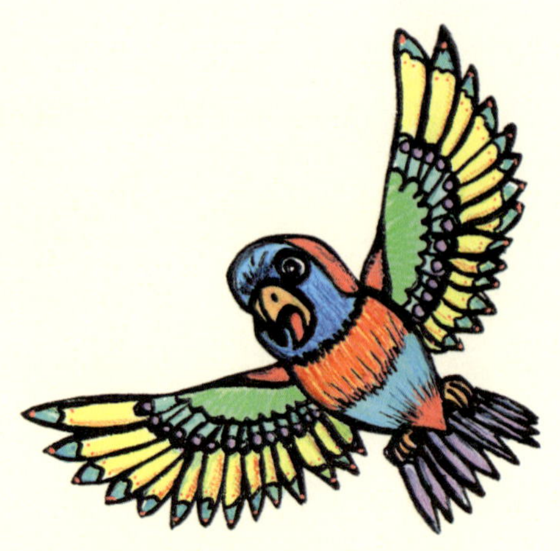

The roos 'ad lots o' talent,
they 'ad spread 'emselves around,
the one who played the sax
was stompin' beats upon the ground.
Another on the violin
and one was on the keys,
the roo on double bass
just had me slappin' on me knees.

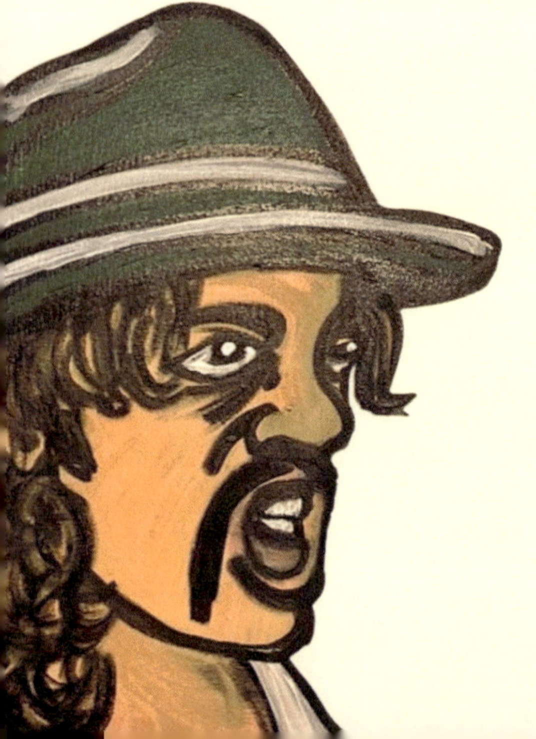

But that's not all I tell yuz,
there was more to it than that,
ya gotta let the missus know
before she smells a rat.
One koala played the cello,
'nother on the squeeze box,
just wait ta hear the next bit
it'll knock yuz off ya socks.

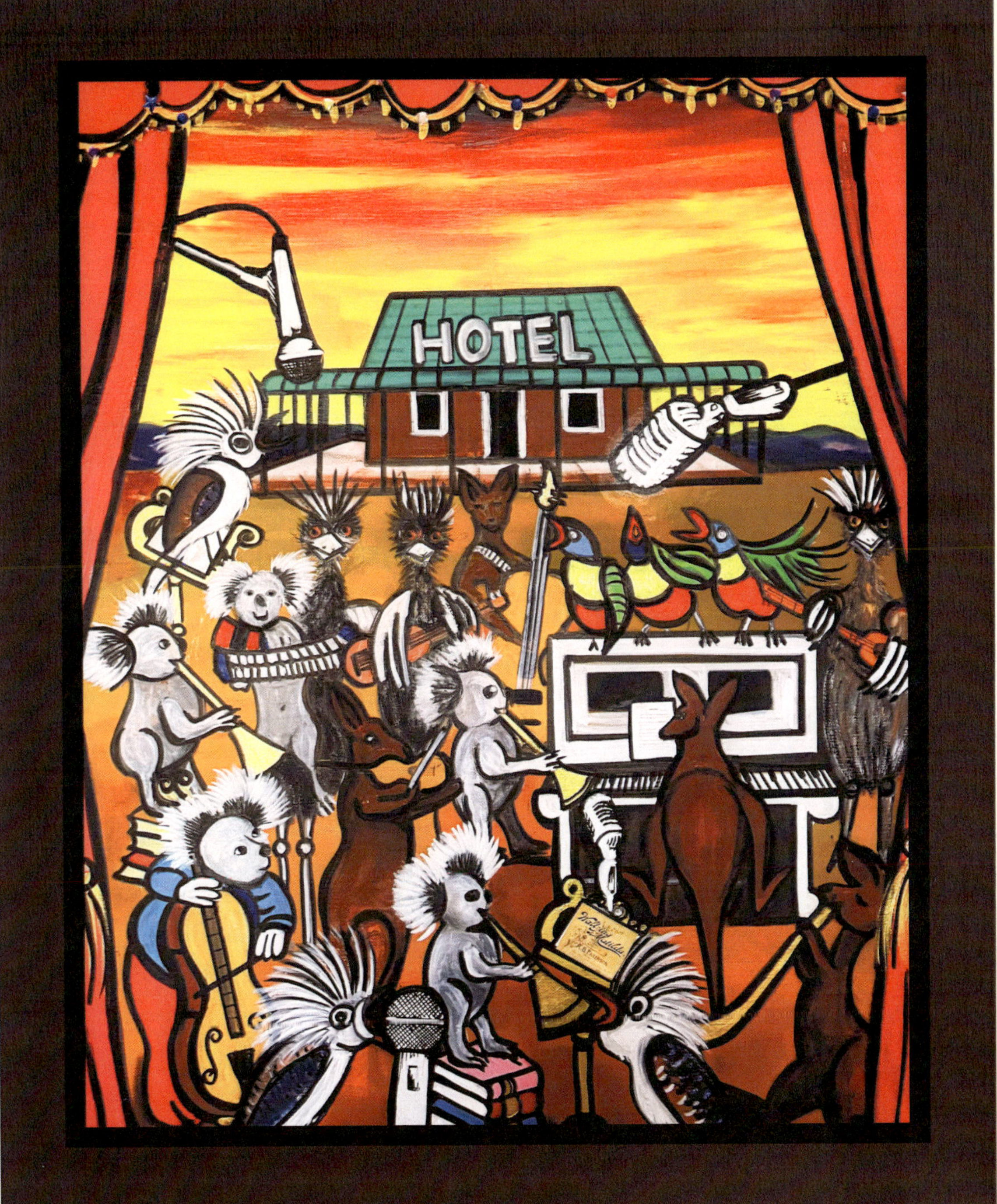

OUTBACK OVERTURE

Orchestral

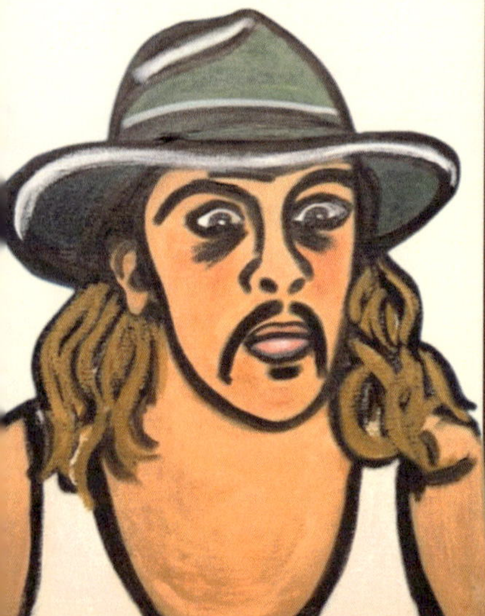

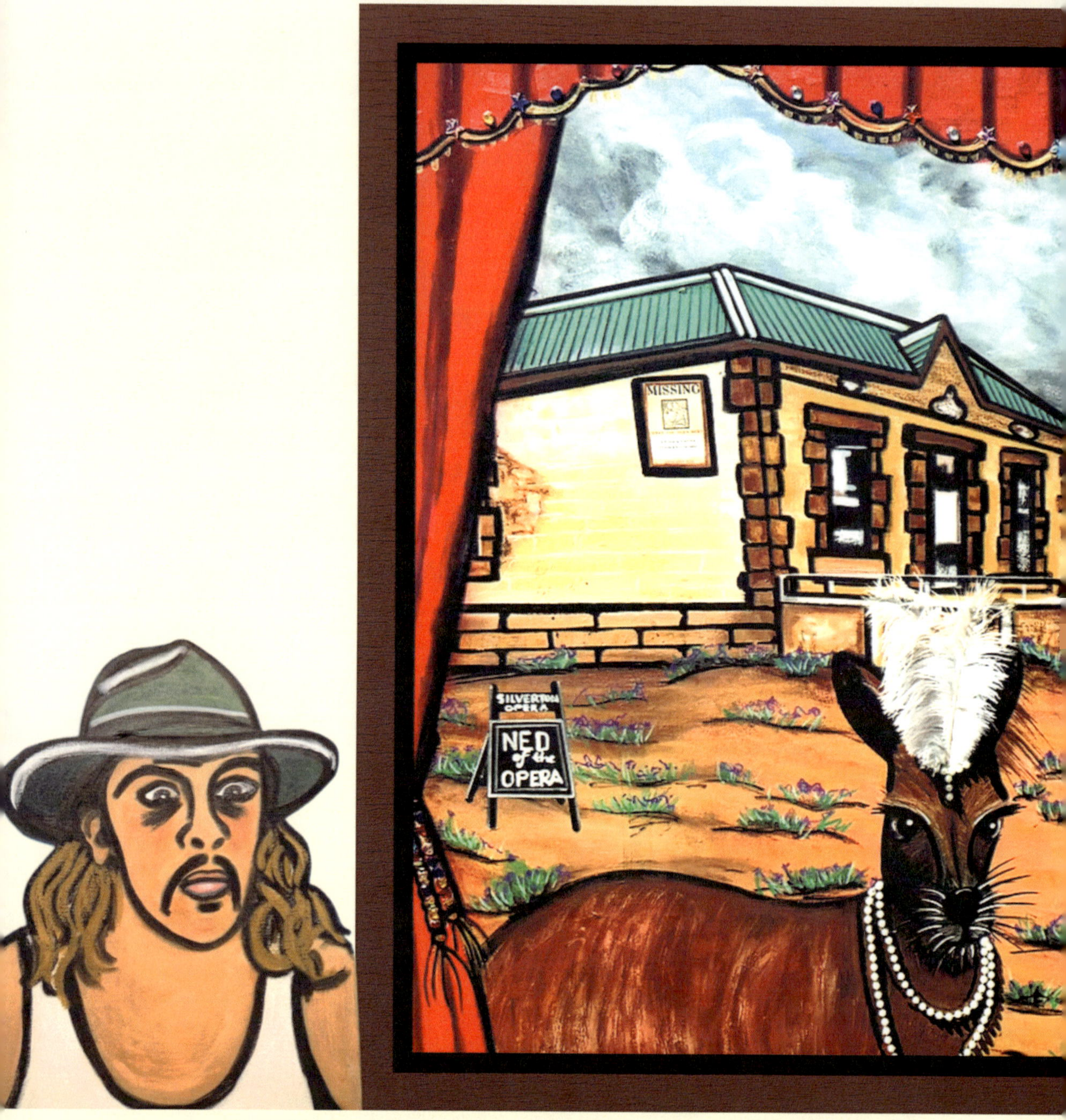

From right o' stage came inta sight a fancy lookin' 'orse,
and on its back Ned Kelly sat, 'is 'elmet on of course.
'E sang a song in op'ra like, that echoed froo the steel,
while movin' left the feathered 'orse tip toed upon its 'eel.

Now up the front, ya can't believe what stared me in the eye,
what 'alf looked like a roo an' 'orse, not tellin' yuz a lie.
I wasn't sure if it was then a sheila or a bloke,
but crikey what I do know is that it fair dinkum spoke.

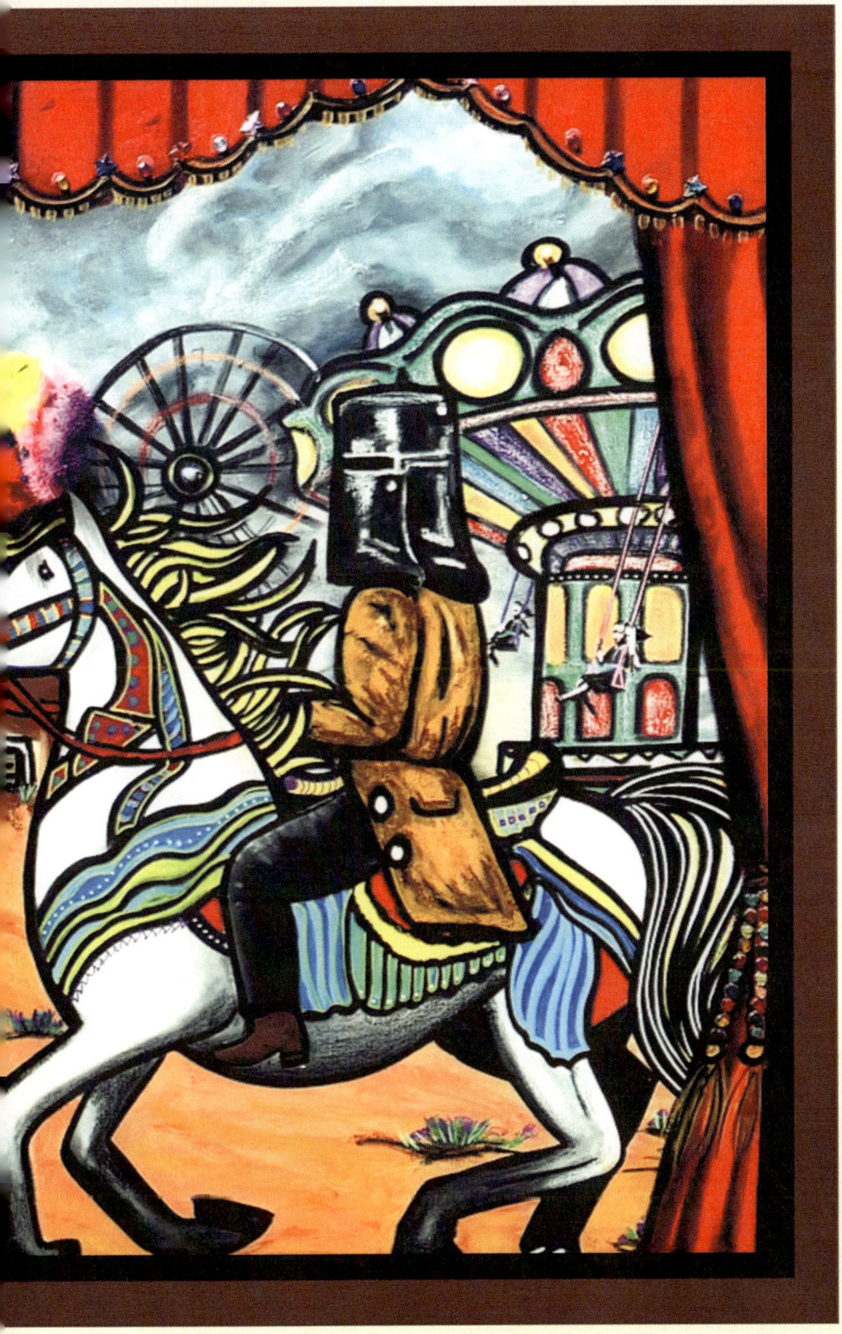

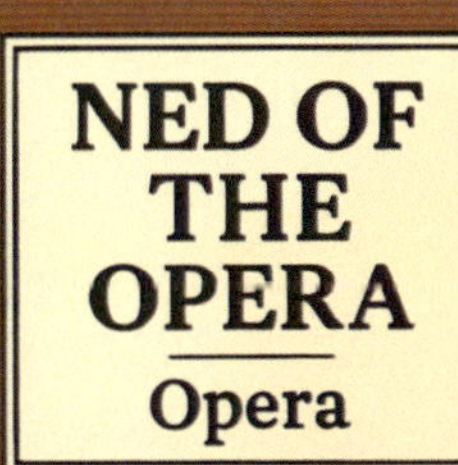

**NED OF
THE
OPERA**
Opera

"Oi you," it said, I looked about and pointed to me chest,
"Yeah you ya little maggot, I'm not talkin' to tha rest."
I took offense to this 'ere brute and grabbed 'im by the gullet,
'e wasn't fazed at all an' yelled, "Rack off ya bogan mullet."

So when me missus wonders 'ow I got this 'ere black eye,
that ratbag of a kangahorse is 'ow when she asks why.
'E grabbed me by the ear and said, "I'll tan your friggin' 'ide,"
I said, "Yeah nah," and took a swing before we went outside.

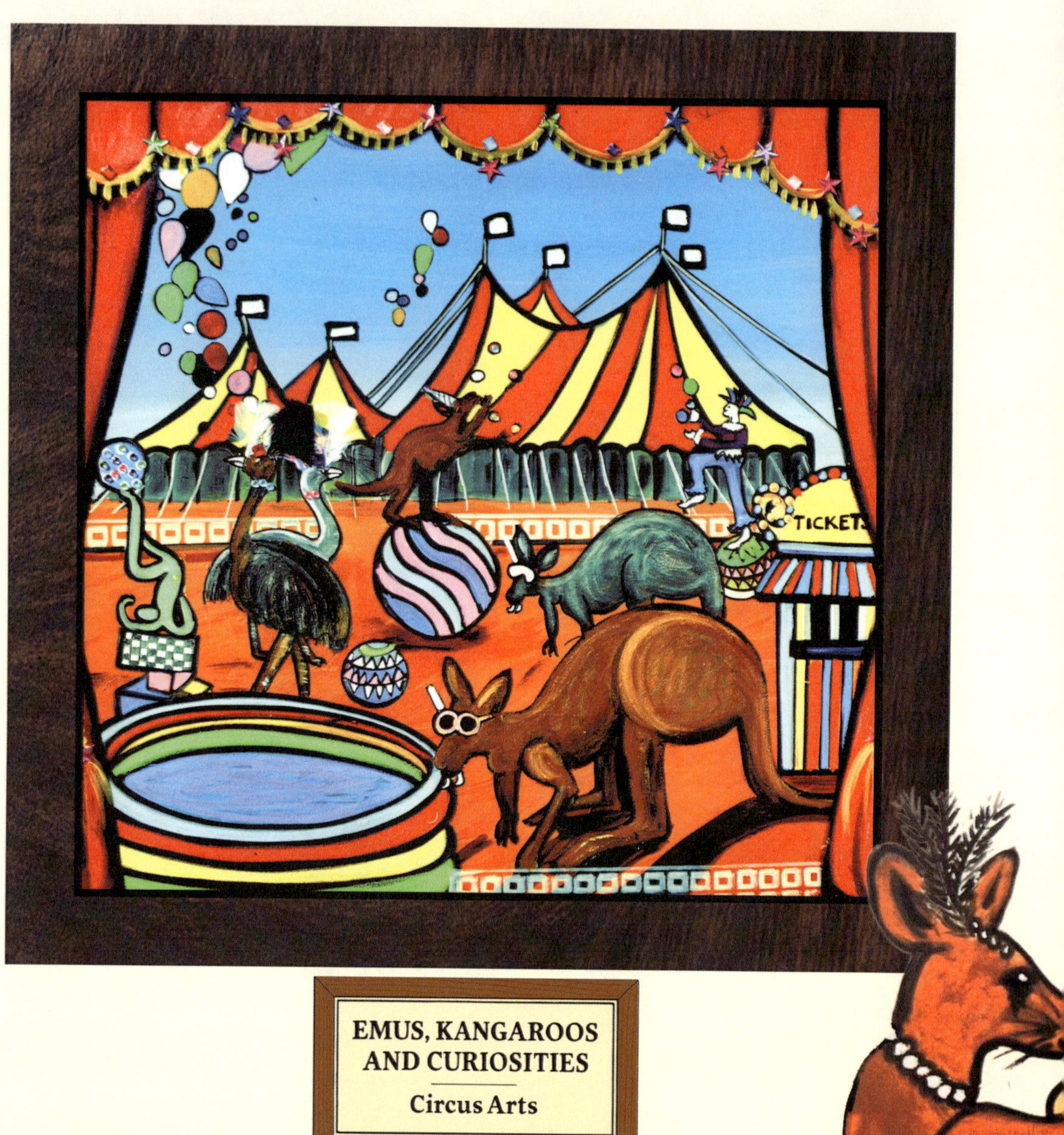

**EMUS, KANGAROOS
AND CURIOSITIES**

Circus Arts

The curt'ns shut 'n open'd up to almost my relief,
the kangahorse still 'ad me ear, just look at this 'ere chief.
'E said, "Yer dumber than the joker there that's jugglin' on the ball,
don't ever show ya face in 'ere next time ya have the gall."

I stood me ground and said to it that "I'm nobody's fool,
I'll bet ya you're too chicken to be jumpin' in that pool."
'E took right up the challenge with a snorkel and some goggles,
next thing ya know 'e shook me 'and, the mind it surely boggles.

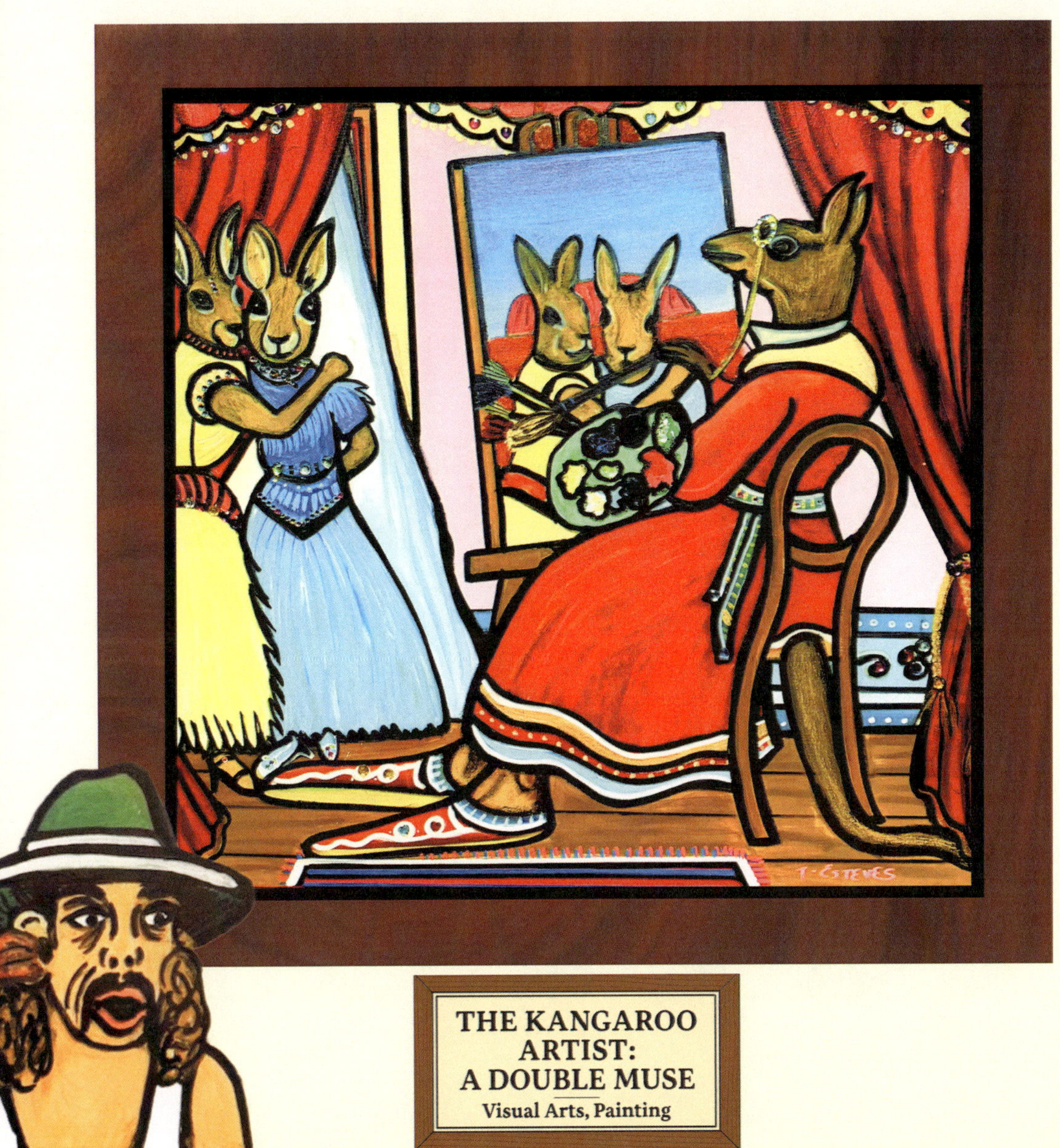

**THE KANGAROO
ARTIST:
A DOUBLE MUSE**
Visual Arts, Painting

'E brought me to 'is grandma's 'ouse and told me she was paint'n,
then pointed out 'is sisters who were ready for some datin'.
I said that "I'm not inta that, as it's against mi practice,
to play up on the missus, else when 'ome I will be cactus."

So say all that when she asks why I ain't been 'ome all mornin',
I reckon she'd be rapt for not awakin' wiff mi snorin'.
The kangathing is now mi mate, I never shot a blow,
'e saddled there right next to me as we boaf watched the show.

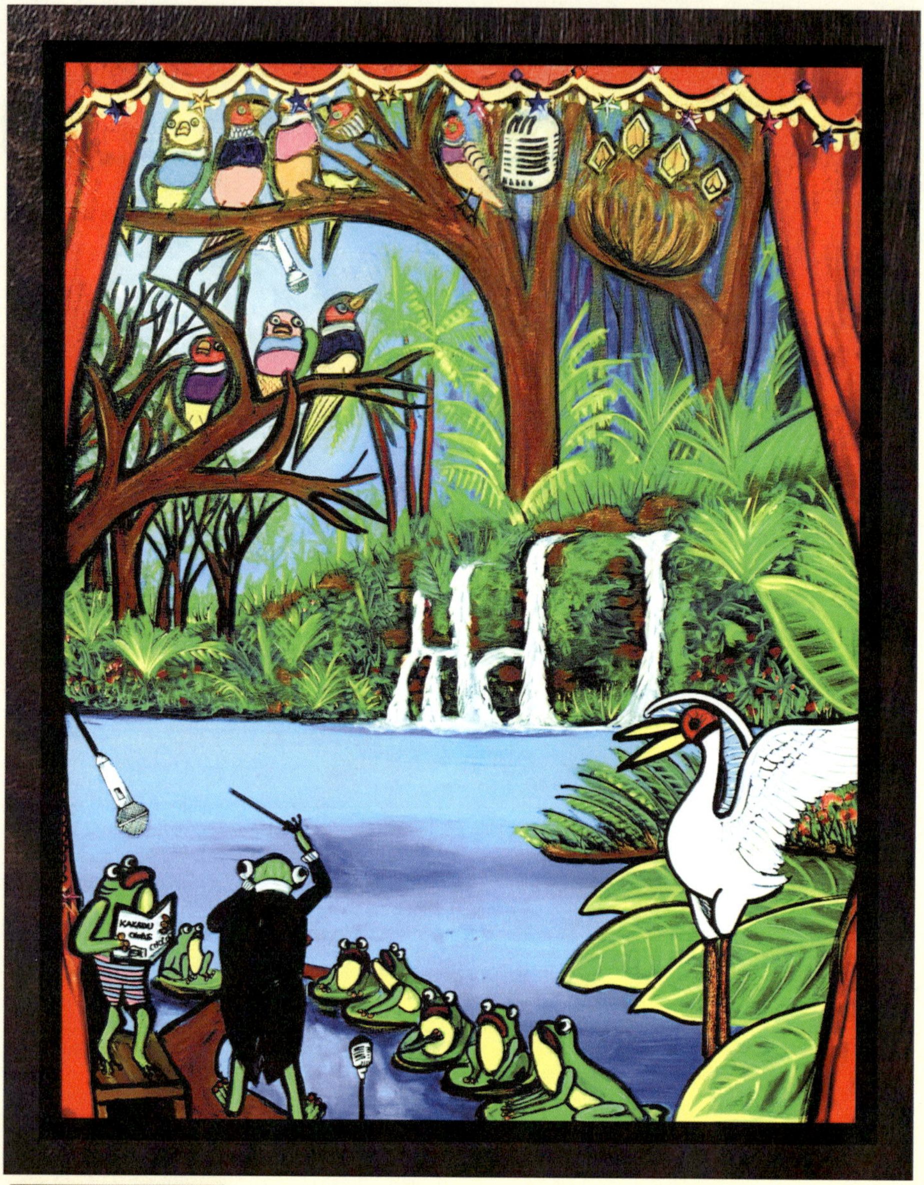

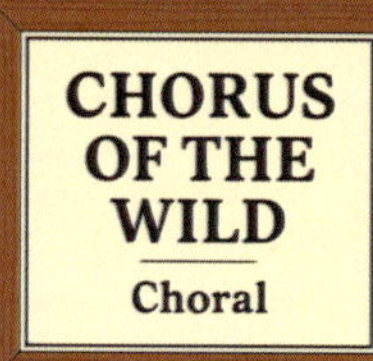

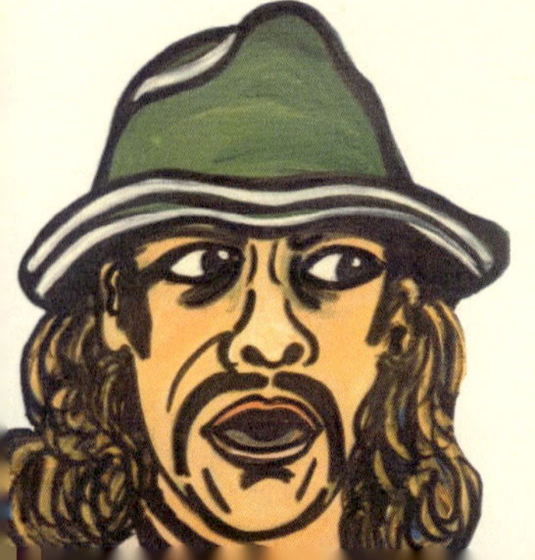

Next thing yuz know the stage was full,
the show it moved along,
in front o' me were coloured budgies,
in a billabong.
And down below some frogs were singin',
true as I have told ya,
and flappin' on the right-'and side
appeared that skinny brolga.

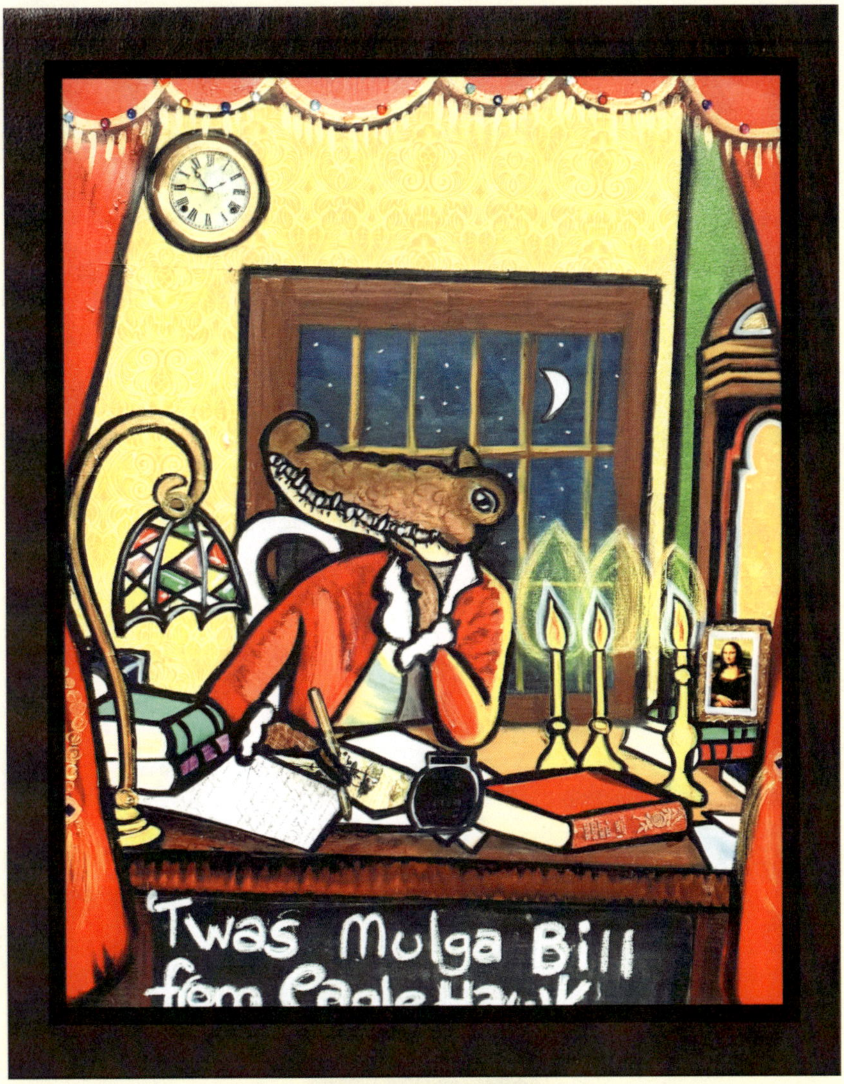

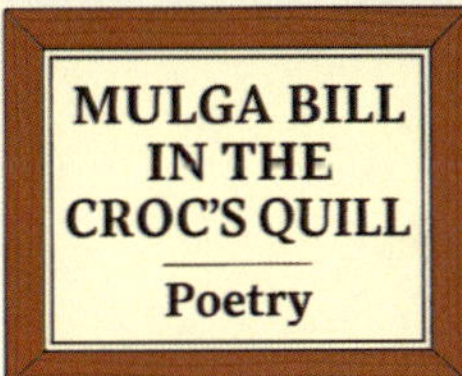

**MULGA BILL
IN THE
CROC'S QUILL**
Poetry

The last bit of the show will have ya skin all in a crawl,
it may provide some insight inta who began the brawl.
A croc recited poetry on stage by candlelight,
and this is where the whole darn set got ready for the fight.

The croc then scanned the audience while writin' with 'is claws,
imaginin' the lot of 'em were snapp'd up in 'is jaws.
He looked at us and said, "Oh my you tasty little bunch,
I reckon I'll just come down there and eat yuz all for lunch."

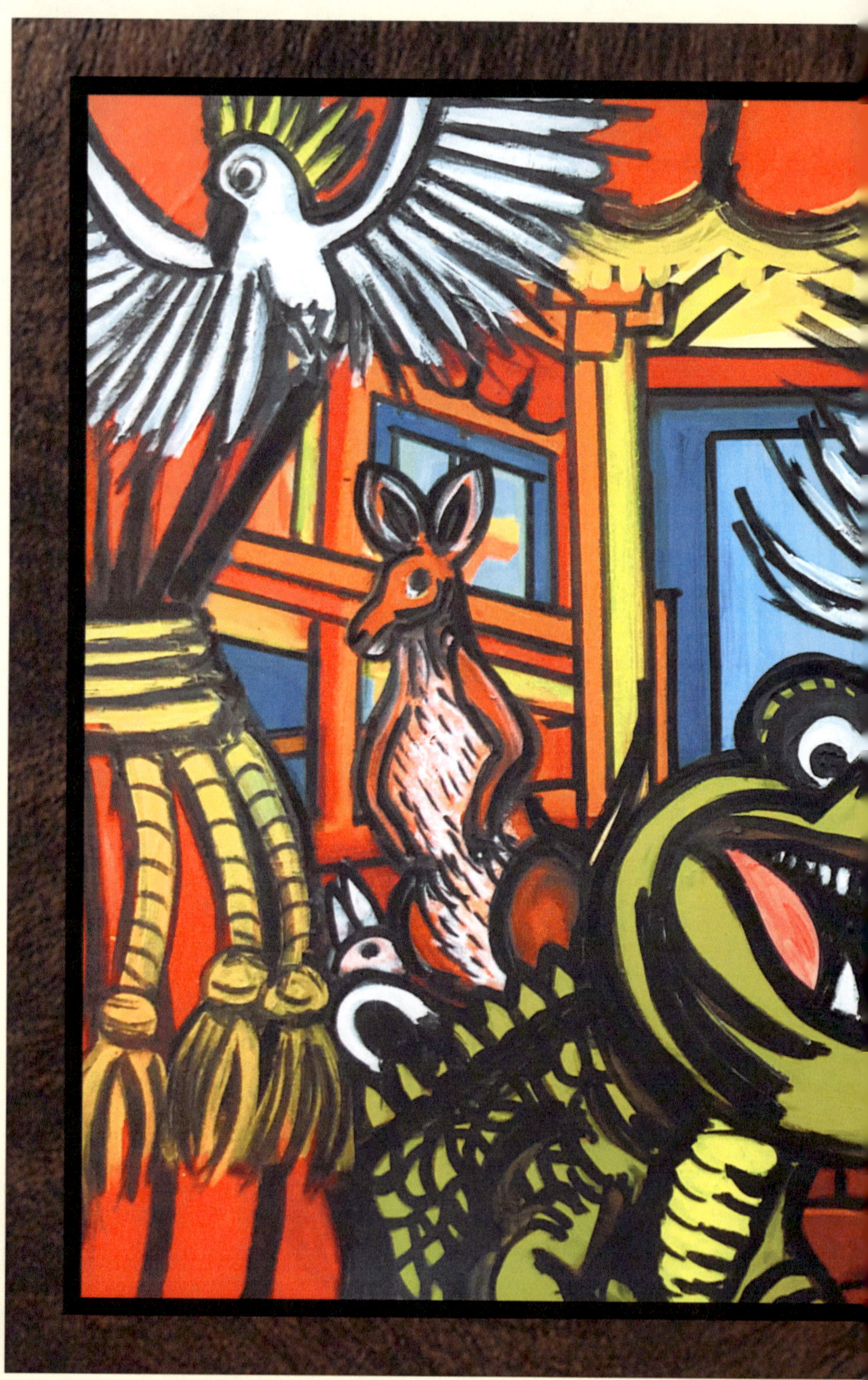

**STAGE
FRIGHT**

Acting

So everybody scrambled, runnin' left and runnin' right,
the croc was chasin' everythin' that moved within 'is sight.
Now when me missus gets all aggro, as I surely guess,
that croc's to blame for putting me in this 'ere friggin' mess.

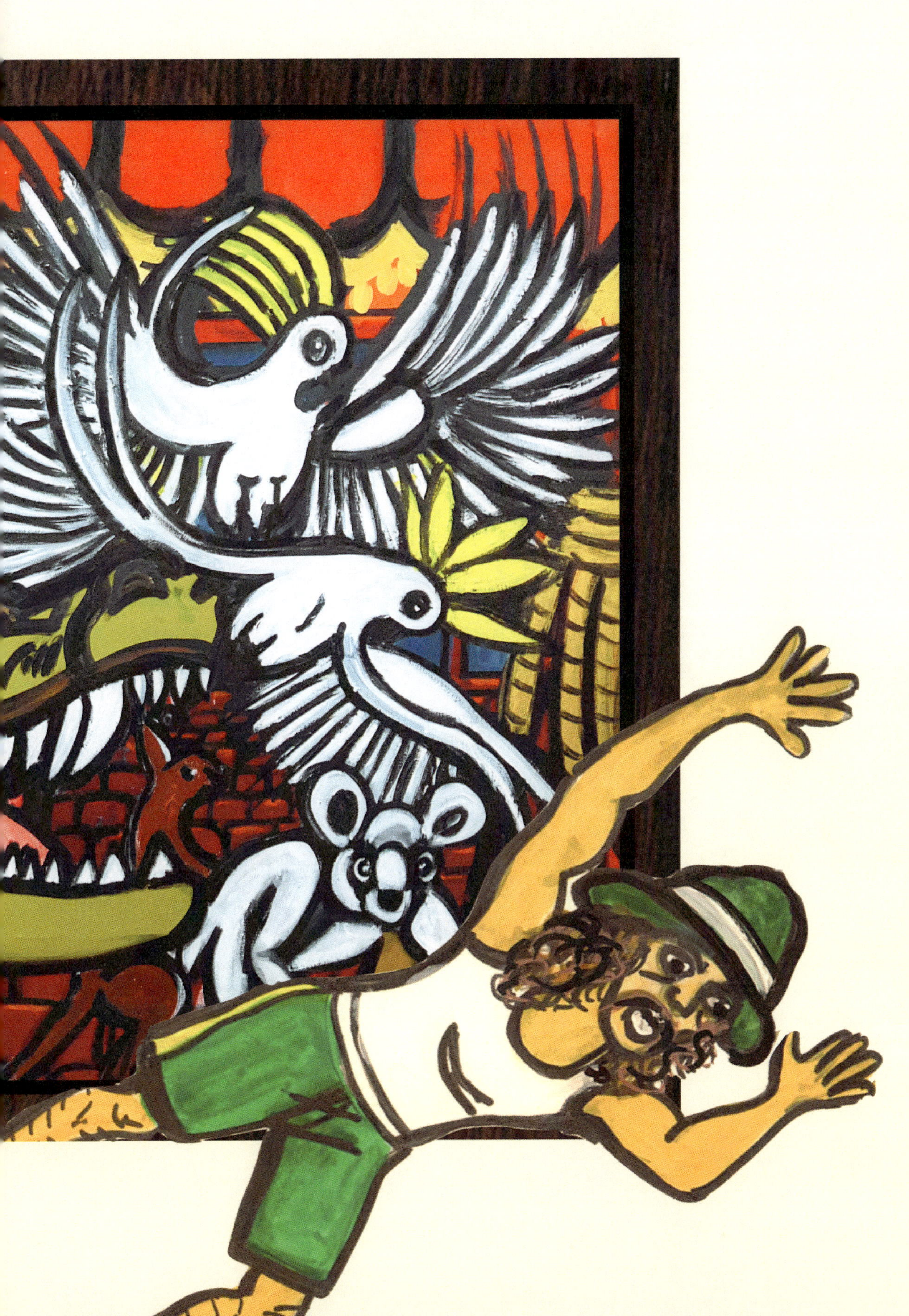

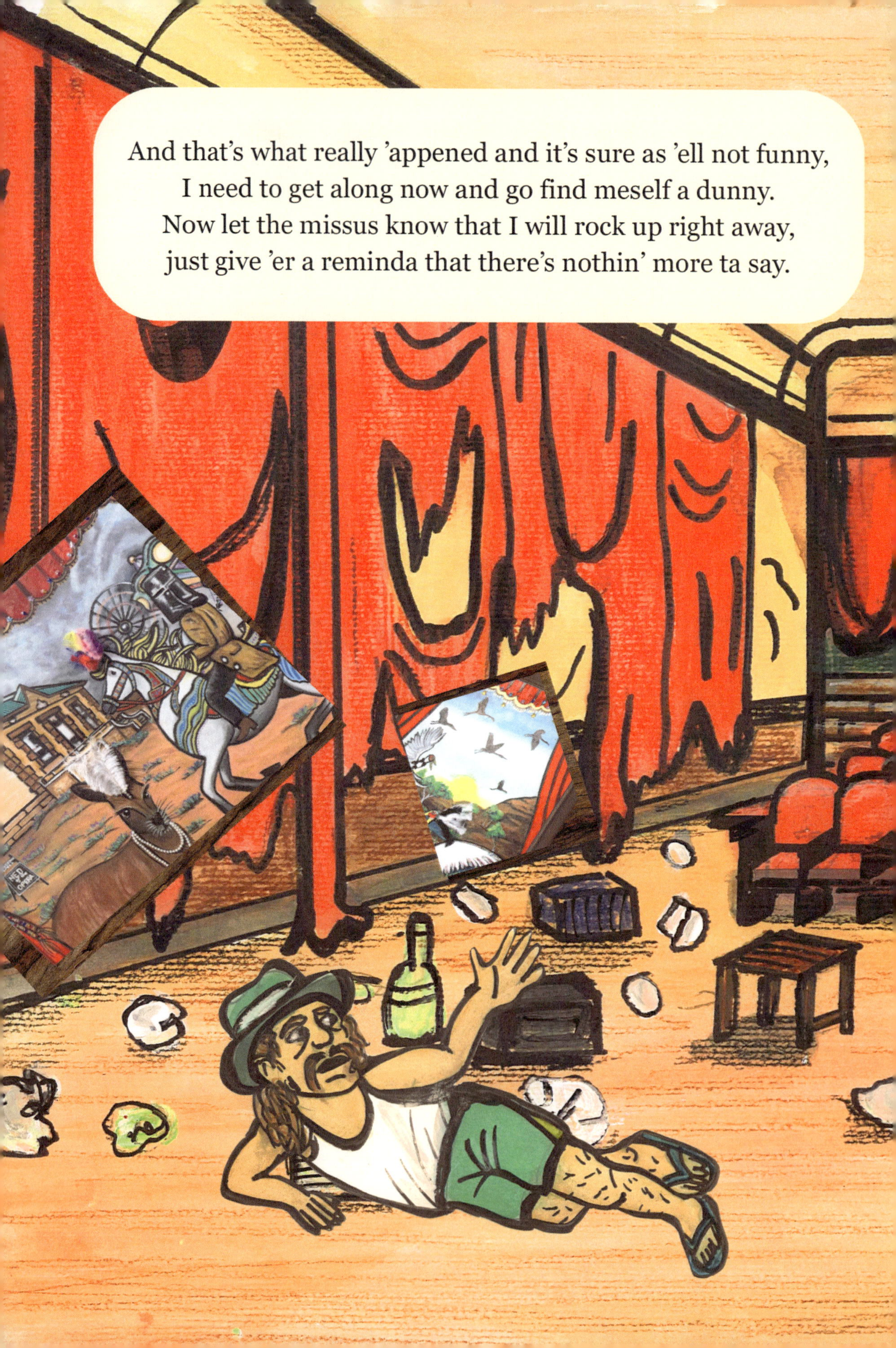

And that's what really 'appened and it's sure as 'ell not funny,
I need to get along now and go find meself a dunny.
Now let the missus know that I will rock up right away,
just give 'er a reminda that there's nothin' more ta say.

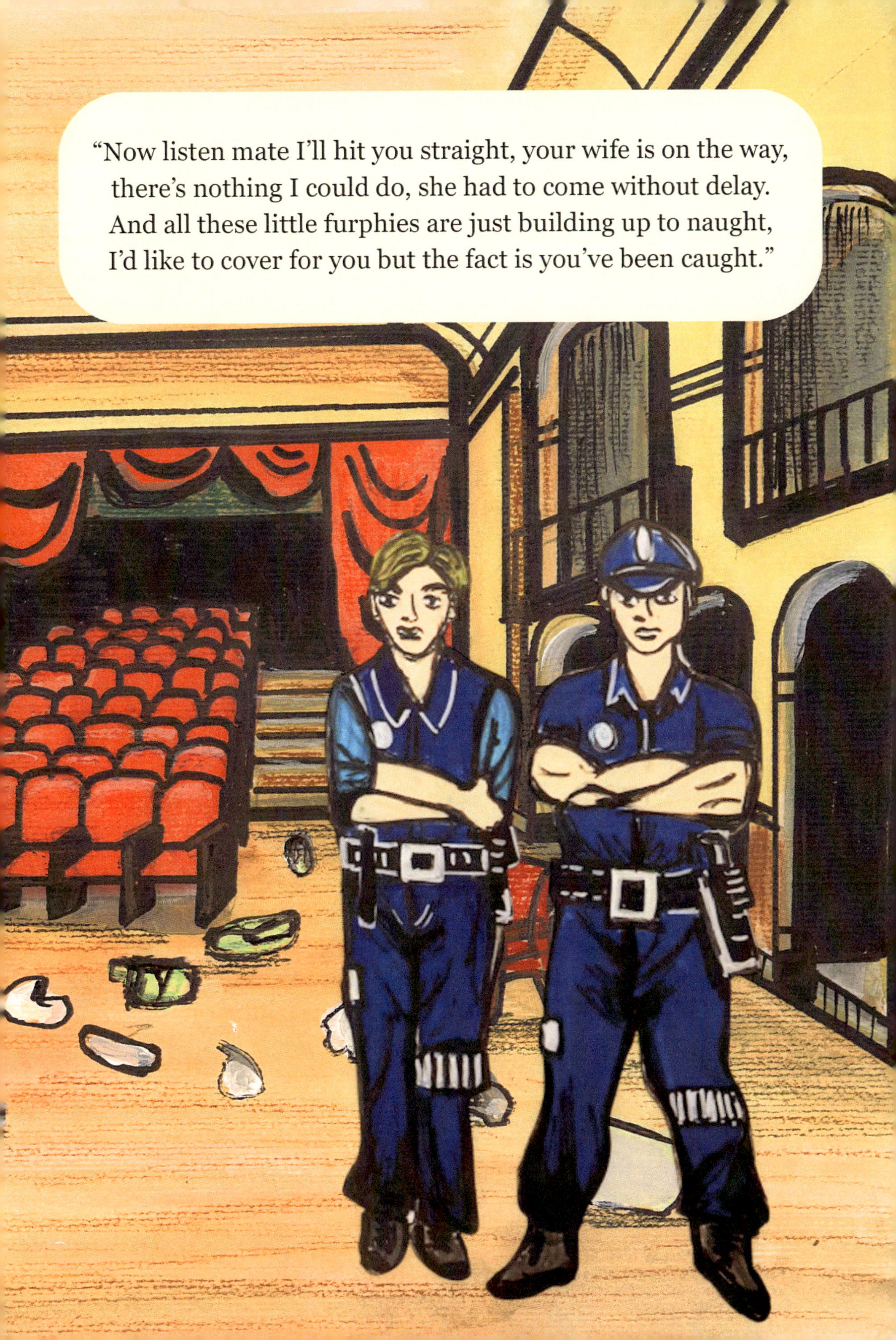
"Now listen mate I'll hit you straight, your wife is on the way,
there's nothing I could do, she had to come without delay.
And all these little furphies are just building up to naught,
I'd like to cover for you but the fact is you've been caught."

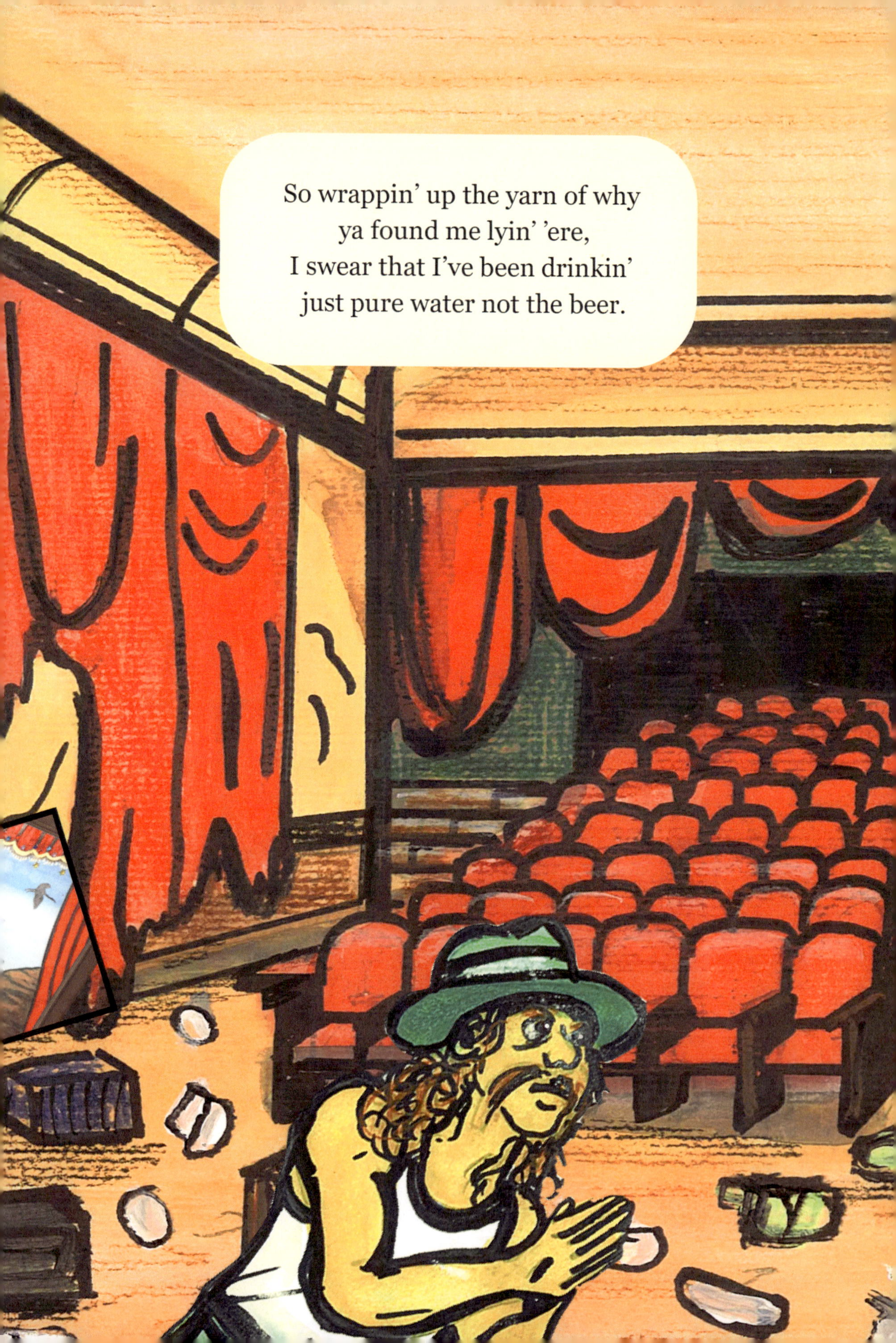
So wrappin' up the yarn of why
ya found me lyin' 'ere,
I swear that I've been drinkin'
just pure water not the beer.

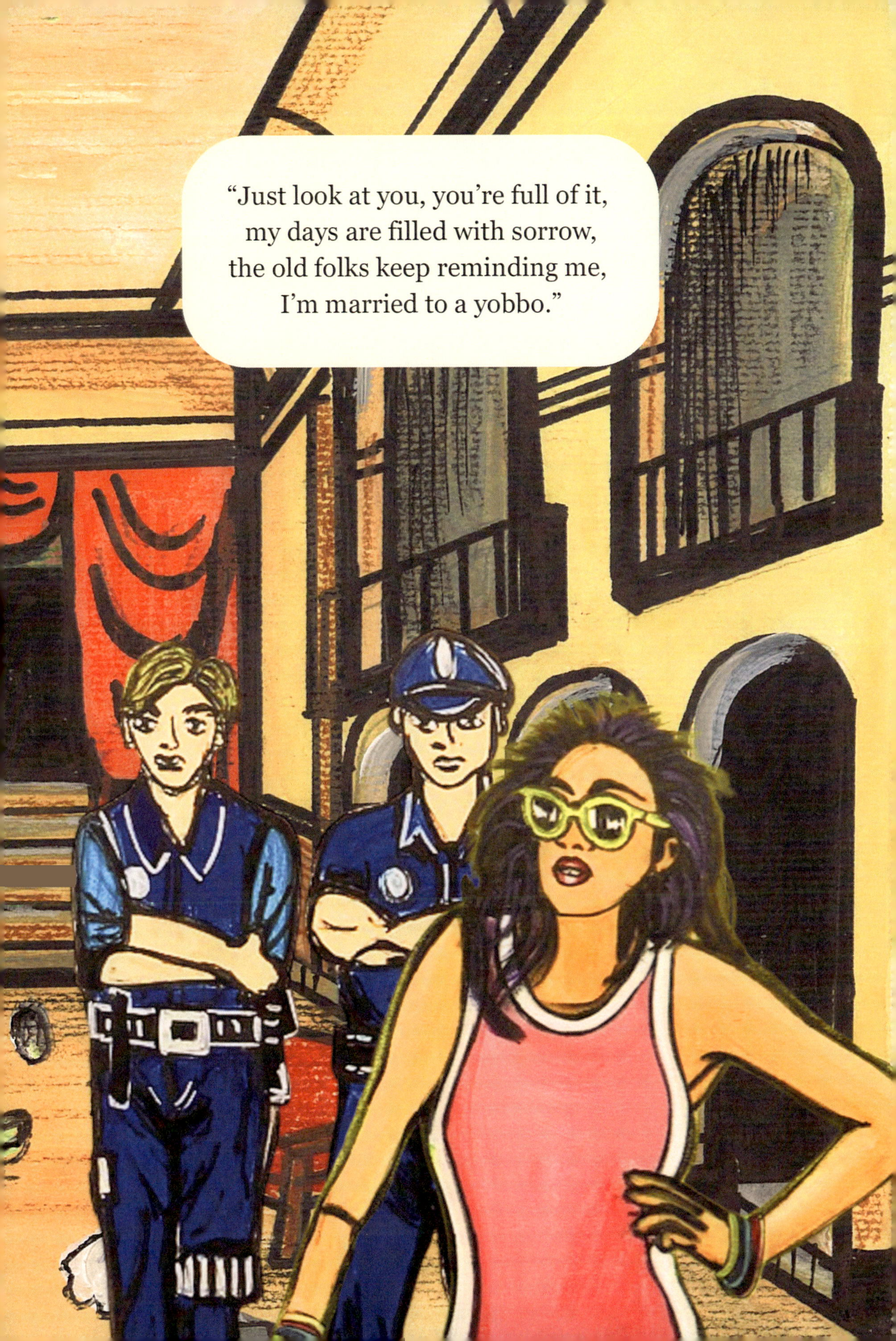

"Just look at you, you're full of it,
my days are filled with sorrow,
the old folks keep reminding me,
I'm married to a yobbo."

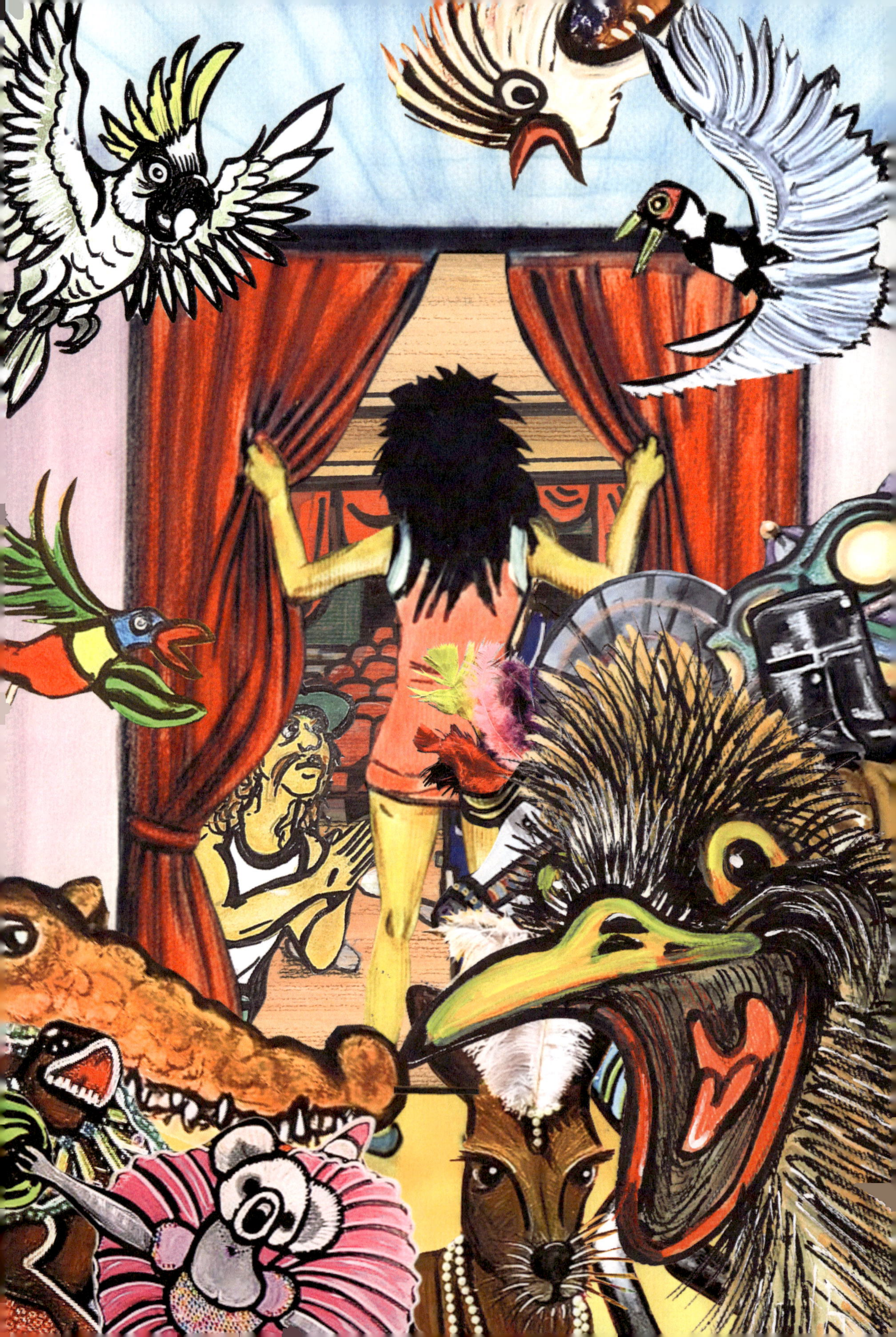

GLOSSARY

G'DAY - Casual greeting, said in a quick and relaxed fashion.

YUZ - Short version of the nonstandard youse.

MISSUS - Wife or girlfriend.

STONE THE CROWS - Old fashioned exclamation of surprise or shock.

YARN - The narrator is spinning a yarn by telling a long elaborate story. It also means to have a chat.

CROOK - Sick or unwell.

LET THE SHOW BEGIN

STREWTH - (strooth) Exclamation of surprise, disbelief or dismay.

BIG RED - Aside from its literal use here, the name has several meanings and evokes a deep spirit of the Australian outback. It is also a nickname for the Red Kangaroo: Australia's largest marsupial.

READING AND LITERATURE

YACK - Trivial conversation.

SCARY SWOOPIN' BIRD - Referring to the Australian magpie.

COCKY - Cockatoo.

BILBY - A nocturnal marsupial.

BOOBOOK - Type of owl.

CINEMA AND MOVIE-MAKING

BUSH TELLY - Bush television: a campfire.

BALLET

CHOOK - Chicken.

DANCE

BLUE - Argument or fight.

BROLGA - A large crane known for its elegant dancing.

CONTEMPORARY DANCE

DAKS - Pants.

MUSICAL THEATRE

HIT FOR SIX - Being floored or stunned. In cricket, six runs is the score from one ball that's hit clean over the boundary fence.

CRIKEY - Exclamation of surprise.

SHEILA OR A BLOKE - Woman or a man.

FAIR DINKUM - Has multiple meanings depending on context and tone. In this case it is an expression of genuine truth.

ORCHESTRAL

RAINBOW LORIKEET - Brightly coloured parrot.

OPERA

NED KELLY - An infamous outlaw and icon of Australian folklore. He wore an iconic helmet with a narrow slit for vision.

RACK OFF - Blunt way to tell someone to go away.

BOGAN - An uncultured, uncouth person. Often (but not always) working-class; tone can be pejorative or humorous.

YEAH NAH - A polite way of saying no.

VISUAL ARTS

CACTUS - Something broken, useless or finished.

RAPT - Thrilled or delighted.

SHOT A BLOW - Threw a punch.

CHORAL

BUDGIE - Australian budgerigar: type of small parakeet.

BILLABONG - Waterhole.

POLICE AND WIFE

DUNNY - Toilet.

FURPHIES - Rumours or stories, especially ones that are untrue or absurd.

YOBBO - Someone who is crude and noisy. Refers to behaviour as opposed to bogan, which suggests a lack of style and class.

DERO - Also derro. Short for derelict, to refer to someone as an unkempt tramp, hobo or bum. See next page.

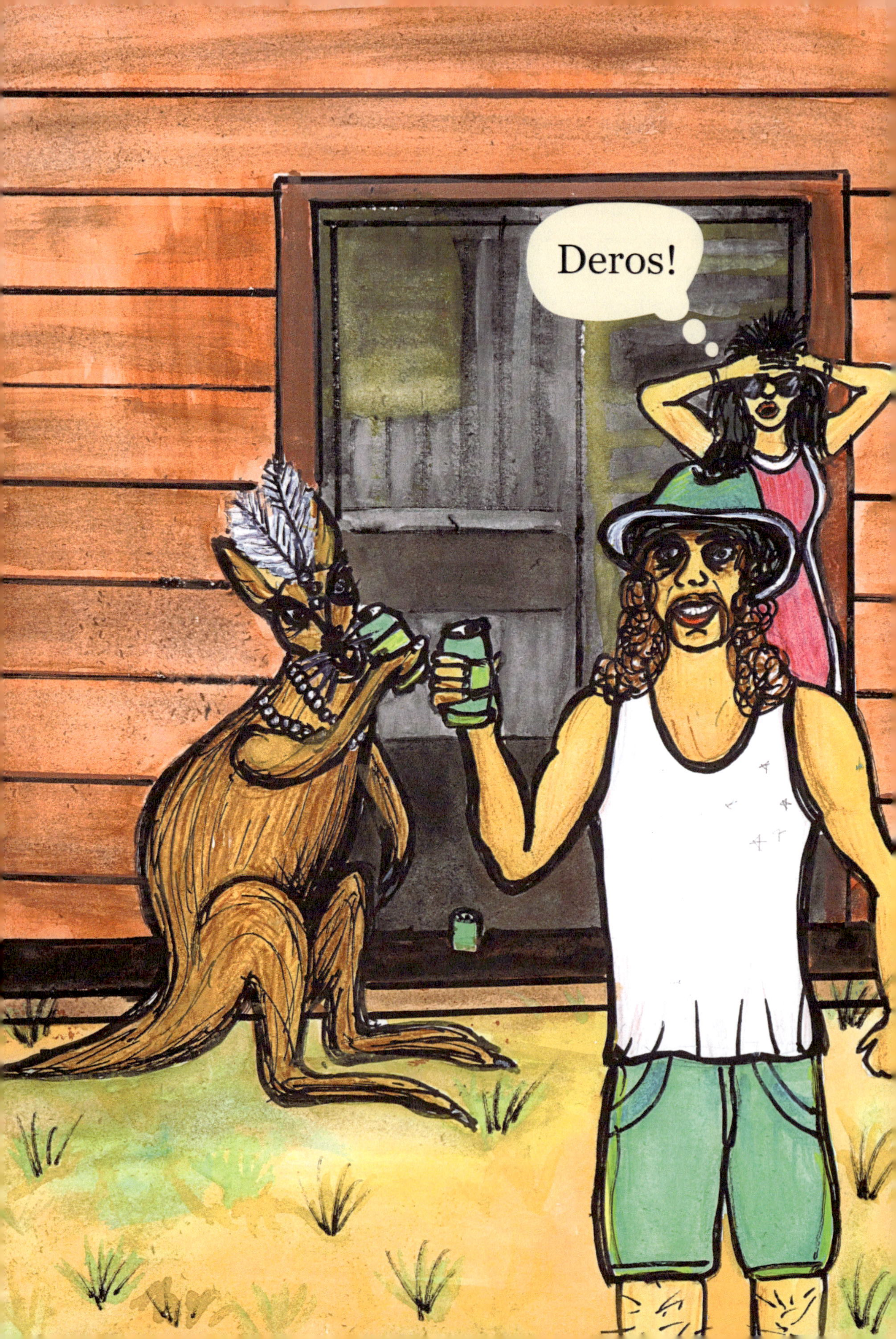
Deros!